**New Directions for
Teaching and Learning**

Catherine M. Wehlburg
EDITOR-IN-CHIEF

From Entitlement to Engagement: Affirming Millennial Students' Egos in the Higher Education Classroom

Dave S. Knowlton
Kevin Jack Hagopian
EDITORS

Number 135 • Fall 2013
Jossey-Bass
San Francisco

From Entitlement to Engagement: Affirming Millennial
Students' Egos in the Higher Education Classroom
Dave S. Knowlton, Kevin Jack Hagopian (eds.)
New Directions for Teaching and Learning, no. 135
Catherine M. Wehlburg, Editor-in-Chief

Microfilm copies of issues and articles are available in 16mm and 35mm,
as well as microfiche in 105mm, through University Microfilms, Inc.,
300 North Zeeb Road, Ann Arbor, MI 48106-1346.

NEW DIRECTIONS FOR TEACHING AND LEARNING (ISSN 0271-0633, elec-
tronic ISSN 1536-0768) is part of The Jossey-Bass Higher and Adult
Education Series and is published quarterly by Wiley Subscription
Services, Inc., A Wiley Company, at Jossey-Bass, One Montgomery Street,
Suite 1200, San Francisco, CA 94104-4594. POSTMASTER: Send address
changes to New Directions for Teaching and Learning, Jossey-Bass, One
Montgomery Street, Suite 1200, San Francisco, CA 94104-4594.

New Directions for Teaching and Learning is indexed in CIJE: Current
Index to Journals in Education (ERIC), Contents Pages in Education
(T&F), Educational Research Abstracts Online (T&F), ERIC Database
(Education Resources Information Center), Higher Education Abstracts
(Claremont Graduate University), and SCOPUS (Elsevier).

INDIVIDUAL SUBSCRIPTION RATE (in USD): $89 per year US/Can/Mex, $113
rest of world; institutional subscription rate: $311 US, $351 Can/Mex, $385
rest of world. Single copy rate: $29. Electronic only–all regions: $89
individual, $311 institutional; Print & Electronic–US: $98 individual,
$357 institutional; Print & Electronic–Can/Mex: $98 individual, $397
institutional; Print & Electronic–rest of world: $122 individual, $431
institutional.

EDITORIAL CORRESPONDENCE should be sent to the editor-in-chief,
Catherine M. Wehlburg, c.wehlburg@tcu.edu.

www.josseybass.com

CONTENTS

FROM THE SERIES EDITOR

About This Publication

Since 1980, New Directions for Teaching and Learning (NDTL) has brought a unique blend of theory, research, and practice to leaders in postsecondary education. NDTL sourcebooks strive not only for solid substance but also for timeliness, compactness, and accessibility.

The series has four goals: to inform readers about current and future directions in teaching and learning in postsecondary education, to illuminate the context that shapes these new directions, to illustrate these new directions through examples from real settings, and to propose ways in which these new directions can be incorporated into still other settings.

This publication reflects the view that teaching deserves respect as a high form of scholarship. We believe that significant scholarship is conducted not only by researchers who report results of empirical investigations but also by practitioners who share disciplinary reflections about teaching. Contributors to NDTL approach questions of teaching and learning as seriously as they approach substantive questions in their own disciplines, and they deal not only with pedagogical issues but also with the intellectual and social context in which these issues arise. Authors deal on the one hand with theory and research and on the other with practice, and they translate from research and theory to practice and back again.

About This Volume

Millennial students (those born between 1982 and 2001) come to our institutions with different needs and experiences than previous generations. Millennial students tend to spend more time with technological gadgets and use them in ways that give them an almost instantaneous response to questions or problems. These students can be frustrating to faculty who might be more accustomed to a different response from students. This volume outlines some practical methods for teaching and learning that can perhaps be used by faculty to reevaluate pedagogical practices and rethink the norms of a college classroom in the twenty-first century.

Catherine Wehlburg
Editor-in-Chief

Editors' Notes

When the two of us met in 1991, we both were teaching first- and second-year writing courses; we regularly discussed the lack of true student engagement in our courses. Students were excited about their fraternities, churches, political activism, and whether the Memphis Tigers won the previous night's basketball game; yet, they were relatively unmoved by the opportunities provided within their formal educational pursuits. During our time working at Memphis State—now the University of Memphis—we regularly huddled in our basement office in Patterson Hall, lamenting the lack of involvement and conspiring to motivate more substantive intellectual, aesthetic, and emotional connection between our courses and students' lives. Our means to motivate seemed sure: We regulated attention from our students, and we demanded that they be in the right place at the right time with the right set of notebooks; these mid-1990s regulations and demands compelled still, quiet, and focused receptivity.

Over the years, students have changed in their norms, values, and expectations. Our overregulation of old became ineffective with Millennial students. As we came to realize this new landscape created by the unique needs of Millennials, the tenor of our discussions waned from traditional overregulation and reinforcement of hierarchical power structures and grew toward student liberation and engagement of a personalized ego involvement—a level more interpersonally powerful than mere achievement of grades, adherence to syllabus-driven policies, and accumulation of accolades from those in positions of authority. Tradition and overregulation suppress Millennial students' sense of self; suppression contradicts the type of exaggeration of self that we came to value.

Purpose of This Volume

Millennials are those who were born between 1982 and 2001 (Rickes 2009). They began entering the hallowed halls of the academy about 12 years ago. The purpose of this volume is to bring readers into the conversation that the two of us have been having over the course of the past decade, as we continue to find problems in traditional overregulation as a means for teaching this new generation of students. Our deeper approach—an approach that fundamentally occurred at the ego level—is based in passionate action, zeal, enjoyment, flow, and the surprising intellectual rigor that expands from this seemingly loose learning space. This approach

New Directions for Teaching and Learning, no. 135, Fall 2013 © Wiley Periodicals, Inc.
Published online in Wiley Online Library (wileyonlinelibrary.com) • DOI: 10.1002/tl.20058

requires students to see the relationship between self and other in new ways. Aiming to bring this approach to fruition has become a meaningful path for us, as we hope it becomes for the readers of this volume.

Yes, this deeper approach motivates changes at the level of instructional methods, and many chapters of this volume will address those methods; but method change without innovative reconsideration of the implied social contract that reinforces conventional norms of the university classroom will ring thinly with Millennials. Learning will be hindered. Indeed, the college classroom is at the nexus of immense social change. It is a change that Millennial students willingly and emphatically push through. Our choice is either to fight it, thus raising Millennial students' sense of entitlement, or to cooperate with it, finding new avenues and raising to new heights the opportunities for ego-driven engagement. The ideas within this book focus more on organically changing the norms that students and professors have come to expect on a college campus. By changing the norms, inventive ways of learning will emerge.

Theoretical Frame of This Volume

Chapters 1 and 2 delineate concepts and themes that become a strong theoretical base for this volume. Here, we wish to explicate a few more concepts that might enhance an understanding of the book.

Ego liberation and engagement do not simply mean "letting the students run the classroom." Instead, productively affirming students' egos offers new opportunities for deep learning and ever-strengthening intellectual rigor. *Ego* is the term that we use to promote the notion that students should feel entitled to express themselves and their own essence in the classroom. That is, this volume is not overly concerned with the denotative ontology of ego; rather, for us, ego represents a sense of enlightened solutions that allow students to affirm themselves and be affirmed by professors.

Another concept that undergirds almost every chapter in this volume is the notion of positive affirmation through classroom relationships, particularly between students and the professor. Through relationships, authoritarian and dominant tendencies of professors are lessened. For instance, this volume lends no credence for professorial attempts to create compulsions by holding grades, scholarships, or other credentials over a student's head as a point for manipulation. Similarly, the many ideas in this volume encourage students to set aside their own sense of entitlement in order to better capitalize on opportunities for engaging themselves by becoming a part of the enterprise of learning in college classrooms. Faculty and students share responsibility for the patterns of entitled student behaviors now seen in higher education classrooms. Both the professor and Millennial student have draconian and empathetic powers upon which they can act.

NEW DIRECTIONS FOR TEACHING AND LEARNING • DOI: 10.1002/tl

Relationships support the types of empathy to which meaningful learning aspires.

What is Millennial about the notion of ego and these relationships that surround it? For professors, Millennial thinking is a new realism of understanding students and classroom relationships as a glass-half-full proposition. The mere conscious acknowledgment of student ego is what creates the Millennial professor. To be sure, as many of the chapters in this volume point out, this new realism and acknowledgment can be uncomfortable for both professors and students, as the classroom routines, productivity tools, and communication norms often conflict with our deeply ingrained experiences; but both realism and acknowledgment can propel a stronger unity between a student's very definition of the self and learning processes. For these reasons, the theoretical call of this volume is clear: to realize and acknowledge the value of the change that is advocated within these pages.

Overview of the Chapters in This Volume

One of the many things that is exciting to us about this volume in the New Directions for Teaching and Learning series is that the various contributing authors all share a common trait—they define themselves as "teachers" at an ego-engaged level. Teaching is not something that they "do"; it is a part of who they are.

Theory and Empiricism. This volume begins with two theoretical chapters and one empirical chapter. In Chapter 1, Kevin Jack Hagopian brings insights into the process of rebuilding a classroom milieu from dysfunctional convention toward something that can be, as he notes, "an intellectually enchanted space."

Whereas Chapter 1 focuses on the classroom space, Chapter 2 focuses on the psyche of Millennial students. In that chapter, Dave S. Knowlton contrasts a psychology of ego entitlement with one of ego engagement. The chapter provides broad structures for moving students toward ego engagement.

In Chapter 3, Darren S. Fullerton reports the results of focus groups with Millennial students. In this chapter, readers learn about students' sense of entitlement as customers of their college or university.

Practice and Application. The next nine chapters provide guidance for professors who want to productively engage students' egos and become more aware of the role that ego plays in the learning experiences of Millennial students. In Chapter 4, Mark Canada helps readers see that the syllabus can bring a course to life for Millennial students—helping the student engage with the course content and its processes in meaningful ways, even as the course is just getting started.

In Chapter 5, Stephen Lippmann shares numerous during-class practices that can fundamentally engage Millennial students' egos. The type of engagement that he describes is not one of pandering; his practices appeal to the pacing that Millennial students have come to expect, and bring focus to ideas that allow for individualized connections with course content.

In Chapter 6, Karen Kelly addresses the issue of "disciplinary thinking" as a means of ego engagement. She shares her design and implementation of an assignment that engages nursing students in the world of political activism. Such an assignment penetrates students' egos by taking them outside of their own expertise and educational interests. While her specific context is nursing, her chapter concludes with advice for faculty members across the academy.

In Chapter 7, Alison G. Reeves shares her approach to using narrative pedagogy by requiring students to create autobiographical digital stories. This chapter provides vivid insight into a process that entices self-revelation from students. Ironically, through self-revelation, Millennial students are provided with an entry point for transcending a self-indulgent commitment only to themselves.

In Chapter 8, C. Michael Elavsky addresses the use of social media in large classrooms. Specifically, he focuses on media-driven lectures that allow PowerPoint and other presentation software to become more of an impetus for soliciting student participation. The chapter also describes the use of Twitter as a medium for providing a complimentary forum to supplement during-class discussion. As a final use of social media, Elavksy describes how he requires students to use virtual bulletin boards and Google applications for out-of-class communication.

In Chapter 9, Heather M. Knowlton provides techniques for interacting with students outside of class. The techniques described in this chapter promote cogent and honest relationships between professor and student. They also frustrate Millennial students' tendencies toward self-proclaimed entitlements by offering strategies for putting students in psychological check.

In Chapter 10, Jonathan J. Cavallero addresses the important topic of social justice. His chapter provides insight into establishing and maintaining a focus on unfairness, bias, and privilege. His approach is far from perfunctory, as he emphasizes the importance of meaningful relationships, personalization techniques, and a mission of combatting student cynicism. Pointing specifically to service learning, Cavallero offers an approach for empowering students toward charity and compassion.

In Chapter 11, David R. Coon and Ingrid Walker provide approaches that shift assessment away from measuring a student's performance and toward creating a sense of classroom citizenship. This sense of citizenship distracts Millennial students from a constricted focus on simply earning a grade and refocuses them, instead, on learning processes.

In Chapter 12, Bruce W. Speck offers a more in-depth look at the professor's ownership in perpetuating notions of entitlement in the classroom. Explicating notions of professorial authority, he provides important points for all professors and administrators to consider as they work through the difficult conceptual issues presented in this volume.

Conclusion

Millennial students' assumptions, beliefs, and behaviors have caused the two of us to revisit many of our ideas about teaching. Surprisingly, one conclusion that we have reached is that addressing the needs of Millennial students and their egos has created a setting in which some of our earliest ambitions for a truly engaged classroom could come to fruition. In some ways this book is a moment in the history of that 20-year conversation that we've been having.

Dave S. Knowlton
Kevin Jack Hagopian
Editors

Reference

Rickes, P. C. 2009. "Make Way for Millennials! How Today's Students Are Shaping Higher Education Space." *Planning for Higher Education* 37 (2): 7–17.

DAVE S. KNOWLTON is professor of instructional technology at Southern Illinois University Edwardsville.

KEVIN JACK HAGOPIAN teaches cinema studies and media studies at the Pennsylvania State University. While teaching at the University of Memphis, he was the first winner of the University's distinguished teaching award.

1

This chapter provides a structural architecture for reducing ego-based conflict in the college classroom.

Rethinking the Structural Architecture of the College Classroom

Kevin Jack Hagopian

How bad has it gotten in your class? Students eating steaming plate lunches, kissing passionately, conducting loud phone conversations, playing video poker? Students refusing to complete group work, ignoring demands to appear for an office session, or using obscenities in e-mails and on evaluations? How about claiming that an undiagnosed learning disability made it impossible for the student ever to attend the class for which she is enrolled? Asking to be excused from class to "barbecue chicken at the go-kart track for a radio station" where the student interned last summer?

The term we use to describe these student behaviors is *entitlement*. It is a word we speak with rolling eyes and shaking head. Anecdotes—all of the above are ones I have witnessed either in my own classes or in classes I have observed—are offered to show that students have grown disrespectful of education, virtually in front of our eyes. This disrespect, we complain, is derived from American society at large. Society's indulgent child-rearing norms, noisome political culture, and sensationalist mass media endorse an ethos of unfocused, confrontational personal expression and selfishness at the expense of personal responsibility and civility (Hedges 2009; Twenge and Campbell 2009).

Entitlement in the Professorial Psyche

For many faculty members, the culture of modern student entitlement is a profound threat. But for some of us, this moment is an opportunity to join students in looking closely at the unquestioned social contract of the

New Directions for Teaching and Learning, no. 135, Fall 2013 © Wiley Periodicals, Inc.
Published online in Wiley Online Library (wileyonlinelibrary.com) • DOI: 10.1002/tl.20059

classroom. Together, we can ask essential questions of this contract: Does it matter? Does this contract arouse, liberate, and then help to shape the intellectual consciousness of the individual student as a learner and a citizen? Or does it merely reenact desiccated rituals of academic order from another century—the nineteenth? These empty rituals are an important aspect of what I refer to as faculty entitlement, or the assumption of a position of social rather than intellectual authority within the classroom. We may feel that such authority is earned by our advanced degrees and appointments, but these are not organically meaningful in the social sphere to our students. Faculty see their course treated as a generic exercise in certification by students who adopt the stylish disengagement and anti-intellectualism modeled by peers; more than anything else, those faculty are angry at being ignored, personally and professionally. Strictly speaking, then, the problem is a *lack* of student ego involvement with the experiences of the course, and we are co-owners of that problem with our students.

A growing culture of self-esteem, arising from indulgent practices in child and adolescent socialization, is widely held to be a character fault of the contemporary cohort of the Millennial college student (Gottlieb 2011; Twenge and Campbell 2009). In our injured view, students import this ethos to college, making our classrooms a site of conflict between the selfish student and the selfless professor (Gordon and Sahagun 2007; Krueger, Vohs, and Baumeister 2008).

But too often faculty feel entitled, as well. Many of them disengage from the life of the individual student in the name of "more important" intellectual projects. This choice mistakenly denies the classroom as an intellectual space and makes inevitable entitled behaviors by our students in response to that denial. Sperber (2000, 112) calls this cycle "the non-aggression pact," a state of détente in which the needs, aspirations, and pathologies of individual learners are ignored so that professors may use the energies conserved to conduct and publish research. In turn, students are tacitly encouraged not to seek selfhood in the classroom, but in the dorms, bars, Greek houses, stadia, and other social spaces of the university (Currie 2004; Moffat 1989).

The various attitudes we designate as student entitlement share two common behavioral effects: They mark student disengagement from the mindful experience of the individual classroom, and they block student capacity to imagine a psychologically enabling relationship with the ideas and experiences of the course. If we truly want an end to the behaviors of student entitlement, then we must also be ready to surrender some of the historical prerogatives of faculty entitlement.

The Foundations of Entitlement in Classrooms

The attitudes we decry as entitlement have been facts in the academy for a long time. Here is how one analyst of American education summarizes it:

There are, of course, students … who take their academic work seriously, but their personal interest is outside the general current of campus approval. The preference and norm on most college campuses is toward maximum exertion in activities and minimum adjustment to academic requirements. Mediocrity is the rule in the classroom. … Only in exceptional cases is [the professor's] real influence more than marginal. … Certainly the structure of academic learning, the limitations of the lecture method, and the formality of interaction between students and faculty aggravate a situation that leads to fence-building, but the situation seems to go beyond a failure of communications. The anti-intellectual values of the students result in hostility, contempt, and suspicion toward the faculty. (Fass 1977, 180–181)

Most of us would consider this an incisive portrait of college students of the 2010s. And it would be, had it not been written about college students from the 1920s. In Fass's brilliant social history of the emergence of an American middle-class youth culture in the 1920s, higher education played a pivotal role in empowering young people, but not in the ways their dismayed faculty preferred. Instead, in Fass's account of that era, college became a social laboratory where young people incubated new gender, sexuality, and class mores. They made visible, often through irrational, transgressive behaviors, the exhaustion they felt at inherited doctrines. For them, college was not the cloistered place where they learned the genteel traditions of previous generations, but a dynamic modern space to discover themselves precisely through opposition to those traditions. Classroom authority was the emblem of those traditions. Thus, students rebelled through "an ethos of hostility toward the faculty" (Fass 1977, 180).

Because Millennial students sometimes enter the classroom expecting it to be a repetition of the habits of high school, they may feel that they already understand the psychological architecture of the classroom. Therefore, it is the world immediately beyond the classroom whose prospect is truly exciting. For those students, the social scene of college is a complex and unpredictable series of vivid encounters with a large new cast of peers. This new and suspenseful social space best signifies the drama of the college experience. The out-of-class social spaces become even more exciting and psychologically overheated with the instant communication and electronic mirroring effects of social media (Turkle 2011). Popular fictional portrayals of higher education such as Tom Wolfe's (2004) novel *I Am Charlotte Simmons* and the film *The Social Network* (Rucin and Fincher 2010) show students impatient with the dull routine of the classroom except when it behaves momentarily as a surrogate for the campus social sphere (Seyforth and Golde 2001).

For Millennial students, most with little experience as independent agents, the perceived liberation they experience within their new peer culture contrasts positively to the rules-based learning economy of the college classroom. From their professors' point of view, they become the resentful adolescents that Keniston (1965) has called "belligerently non-adult," immune to real learning (191).

My years in the classroom have shown me that the mores of college students *have* changed; unquestioned structures of generational and intellectual authority really *have* eroded, and technology really *has* created affordances to turn these disruptions into a visible lack of mindfulness in the classroom. Indeed, not since the 1920s that Fass (1977) writes of have changes in economics, media, and consumer technology combined to destabilize the social contract associated with higher education. Then, too, rising middle-class concerns associated with the costs and values of a college diploma are also generating anxieties. Together with the interrogation of the legitimacy of knowledge that now animates all the humanities, higher education is in three-dimensional tumult (Menand 2010).

Students, like anyone, become frustrated with regimentation. But in addition, they are inexperienced in establishing mature relationships with non–parental authority figures. They live in a media world that overvalues strong personal expression throughout society. For students, the classroom is one of the few places in their new adult life where they may feel confident in acting out their frustrations over that regimentation in ways that have already been validated by popular culture (Frank and Weiland 1997). Perversely, they may even become irritated by our attempts to offer a democratic model of the classroom that is so distinct from their preconceptions of that space that it seems to violate comfortable boundaries between school and self (Cox 2009). That is, much of what we call "entitlement" arises not from an overempowered personality, but an underempowered and frustrated one, seeking autonomy where it may. Or, as an honors student recently said to me, "Every idiotic thing a college student does in class is just another way of saying, 'Hey! Look at me! I'm over here!'"

The Psychological Architecture of Conventional Classrooms

The psyche and history that I have just described have led to a convention of ego entitlement. This convention permeates many college classrooms. The ego-entitled classroom is one in which education is routinized to accord with institutional rather than educational needs. The conventions of the ego-entitled classroom include rigid demarcation and regulatory thinking.

Rigid Demarcation. The conventional college classroom has long been a place where the elements of learning—content, students, professors—are rigidly demarcated. In that classroom, students seek quantitative approval from faculty in the form of grades, while avoiding unique (and hence, impossible-to-quantify) course-based ego engagement with faculty, with content, and with each other.

Not surprisingly, what Ramsden (1992) has referred to as "teaching as telling" is normalized as the main way of doing business in the entitled classroom, not only by faculty, but by students. By contrast to other kinds of demonstrative and experiential teaching discussed by Ramsden, "teaching as telling" is the easiest style to master for a setting in which the focus is on professorial expression rather than student learning. "Teaching as telling" reinforces the student's role as passively centered on an expert recital of professorial subject knowledge rather than student ownership and internalization of the subject matter. As a model of the skilled performance of a subject, an act of cultural interpretation, "teaching as telling" has a place in our retinue of skills; but it has become a default strategy because it validates objective forms of assessment. It defines knowledge as a closed loop that privileges the teacher and textbook.

Regulatory Thinking. Because of rigid demarcation, students may well see their semester as a struggle to fit themselves successfully to the professorial ego. The phrase "I wish she'd just tell us what she wants!" overheard in hallways and seen in text messages between students marks this collision of separate agendas of professor and student. This confrontation becomes normalized over time in the life of professors, too; indeed, it may even be ego-entitling to us, as students seek to divine the unique formula for success from clues carefully parceled out by professors who see themselves as course protagonists.

Serving this pursuit of the mysterious professorial ego by young learners is what I refer to as "regulatory thinking" in the organizational superstructure of the course. Regulatory thinking, like other bureaucratic systems, is contractual, is inorganic to experience, and develops a life of its own that weighs heavily on a person's self-perception (Benveniste 1977).

The course syllabus is one example of regulatory thinking that is particularly contractual. At my university, up to 70 percent of the prose of a course syllabus is taken up with boilerplate language provided by the university on such matters as attendance, plagiarism, and verification of disability status. Universities often see the syllabus not as an agenda for cooperative learning, but as a tool to reduce ambiguities associated with negative student performance, in order to forestall student grade complaints. This bulletproofing is then joined to a methodical calculus for the assigning of course grades in which assignments are broken down into patented rubrics and detailed percentages that range from the tedious to the molecular. I had a colleague whose students' grades were computed on a potential of 5,000 course points. The syllabus is the first formal message students receive from us; and it is often one of regulation, not of personal liberation or intellectual investigation.

Turning qualitative evaluation into quantitative measurement is necessary in education. But the mechanized syllabus is emblematic of how what begins as well-intentioned pedagogy can end as a fetish. In creating a floor of identical conduct beneath students in order to make comparative assessment possible, the syllabus is an example of how classroom practices unconsciously create a ceiling for many students' individual intellectual aspirations.

NEW DIRECTIONS FOR TEACHING AND LEARNING • DOI: 10.1002/tl

Cox (2009) has written of the resentments regulatory thinking induces in both professor and student. For students, these resentments accelerate what she terms the socially based "college fear factor." Cox points to the especially debilitating effects of this "fear factor" for members of groups previously excluded from higher education; these disenfranchised members may not be familiar with the essentially cultural, rather than intellectual, literacies exemplified by the technical language of the standardized sylla-bus. They also may not be familiar with the routine competencies of assess-ment types, such as the multiple-choice exam or the argumentative essay (Cox 2009, 157). These in-group literacies exaggerate the importance of institutional skills for all students. Such pro forma choices immediately separate students from content as the course begins. From these conven-tions comes a learning style that is disembodied and externalized, and thus frustrating to ego engagement.

A democratic classroom by itself cannot counteract the devaluation of education in a democracy. For instance, consider that I teach a large intro-ductory cinema studies course with enrollment up to 450 students. The size of the class makes inconceivable nearly all the teaching suggestions in Bain's (2004) excellent handbook, *What the Best College Teachers Do*. Simi-larly, Berube's (2006) description of the intellectually intimate relationship between professor and student also is not possible in a mass class. Booth's (2003) innovative, iterative assessment techniques and Bruffee's (1999) col-laborative philosophy that undergirds those techniques were designed for smaller classes that are taught by specialist faculty committed to pedagogi-cal growth over the long term, not casual hires or graduate student appren-tices. No reframing of the classroom relationship will be sufficient to redress the decay of higher education that such policy choices make inevi-table (Newfield 2008).

But it *is* possible that a changed, dynamic classroom experience, one in which teachers consider every choice in the light of ego engagement and its offspring—real learning—rather than regulatory thinking and its stepchild—certification—will do more for its 15 million consumers per year than just make them useful, ethical, and creative citizens. The same experience may also re-create them as engaged voices in debates on higher education policy.

A Checklist for Structuring an Ego-Engaged Classroom

In this volume, we make a distinction between the pointless egocentric behaviors we decry as entitlement and genuine ego engagement through the experiences within our courses. An ego-engaged classroom fits Illich's (1983) definition of the classroom as a place that makes the education of an individual possible—not merely a space in which instruction takes place. In the ego-engaged classroom, students understand knowledge as *having to do with them*, and with their establishment of a personal, adult stake in citizenship and the social order.

I advocate a teaching philosophy that generates rather than suppresses ego engagement. Indeed, this engagement is a foundational educational goal. If *ego* is the name we give to the emerging selfhood of the student, then it is time we sought to fuse that selfhood to the subjects we teach. To achieve this fusion, our task is threefold. First, we must use our courses to destabilize student assumptions about one-way intellectual power. Second, we should offer students responsibility for their own education and that of their fellow students. Third, we must call students to invent a new, personalized structure of authority for which intellectual command of and practical transactions with the ideas of the course are fundamental. Collectively, these three will help us build classrooms in which students achieve ownership not merely over the material, but *over themselves as unique individuals*.

The engaged classroom we build in which they can achieve this transformation is an intellectually enchanted space, a place of purposeful choices in learning that work consciously against the default settings of the conventional classroom of entitlement. If the notion of enchantment seems poetic rather than practical, then remember the passions and ideals that first brought you to research and teaching in your field. Isn't this precisely the state of deep engagement that you'd like to achieve in your classroom? The following list can help.

Acknowledge That Entitlement Cuts Two Ways. If it is a problem that students arrive in your classroom carrying unearned assumptions about their privileges as consumers, then it is also a problem when you enter the classroom with assumptions about respect for advanced intellectual accomplishment that students may not share. They simply feel freer to express these attitudes than did previous generations of students. During boring college lectures, I wrote letters; now, students text. Their gadgets, blinking in the darkness of a lecture hall, merely announce their disengagement; they are not the cause of it (Elavsky, Mislan, and Elavsky 2011).

Be Comfortable with "Why Do We Need to Know This?" Students have elected not to keep quiet about their disengagement but, in a rough fashion, to demand an end to it. Though often flip or truculent, students' questions about "Why do we need to know this?" whether asked directly or implied, are legitimate. Professors should look forward to these questions, not dread them. They are an opportunity to create the intersection between self and subject that can give unique meaning to the entire semester's work for a student, and for the students who participate in the conversations that follow. As Booth (2003) has shown, many academic fields can be recast as a search for "personal identity" (41). What begins as an annoying encounter may well end in a student posing a foundational question that provides unique connection between that student and the discipline.

NEW DIRECTIONS FOR TEACHING AND LEARNING • DOI: 10.1002/tl

Importantly, the question of "Why do we need to know this?" is legitimate for professors, too. Indeed, we should raise these questions before our students do, as these questions should be elemental to the metacriticism of our courses. By raising these questions proactively, we provide even broader opportunities for Millennial students to connect themselves to the course.

Understand That Classroom Form also Functions as Content. Students learn something from every detail of the classroom experience, whether professors intend it or not. Some of these features we cannot change—the meeting times of the class, for instance, and some evaluation benchmarks. In other areas, we have considerable latitude. This presents us with opportunities for significant personal imprint. But whether voluntary or involuntary on our part, in each case learning proceeds from each signifier offered in the entire history of the course. Thus, if the preliminary welcoming e-mail we send students orienting them to the class contains typographical errors, students see unprofessionalism normalized, while the "every other seat" arrangement in a final exam space assumes criminality on the part of every student. From first to last, each choice teaches something.

We must be sensitive to the ways in which cultural norms naturalize ideologies not only in the content but in the forms of our courses. Metatheorizing about content is available to the practitioner of any academic discipline that has undergone substantial paradigm conflict in the past generation—that is, almost every discipline (Menand 2010). Students can be an important part of this activity, and in so doing, gain a sense of ownership over the direction of the knowledge in their field. In economics, for instance, the swiftly evolving perspective of behavioral economics, which contrasts the often irrational actions of economic actors with the rationality of market forces, is unusually appropriate both for teaching Millennial students to understand paradigm change in economics and locating the study of economics in their own irrational behaviors (Becker 2000).

I require students in film studies courses to make short films and then submit them to the class for analysis. This requirement brings the challenges "real" filmmakers face into close view, because students have become real filmmakers and real critics. This strategy also intellectually legitimizes the kind of creative work in the arts that students of all interests now routinely do outside of class. Through this strategy, students learn something valuable about the power and ethics of criticism of their work. The experience of receiving any kind of criticism (including mine of their written work) extends far beyond anything I could merely tell them (Selber 2004).

Rethink Disciplinary Thinking. Commonly, the task of a university professor is to help the student "think like a sociologist"—or an economist, film historian, biologist, linguist, or whatever (McConachie and Petrosky 2010). But in practice, "thinking like" is often presented as a kind of theater, a hermeneutic performance of arcane information by the professor, accompanied by readings from the professional literature originally designed for the consumption of practitioners, which are then decoded by the professor.

Distinguish those features of your field that are actually marks of productive intellectual specificity from those discourses and habits that are merely professional conventions, and thus extraneous to true disciplinarity (Hacker and Dreifus 2010). That activity should hurt a little, because those conventions are just as dear to us as the next text message from a BFF is to our student. It may be possible, for instance, that the academic journal articles that we and our colleagues write, with their rarefied diction and lengthy references to internecine debates within the discipline, may not always be the most intellectually useful reading material for the rookie and the nonspecialist (Gallagher 2008; Geisler 1994; Nelson 1986).

A course I recently taught in comedy film began with a historical overview of the comic cinema—a disciplinary narrative that my students found resolutely unfunny. They were direct in expressing their frustration, and it led to an entirely new avenue of inquiry in which, as a group, we analyzed violence as an ironically comic and socially subversive trope in the contemporary cinema. Under my guidance, we went back through cinema history to recover numerous instances of this perverse juxtaposition. And students created a link between this history and their own popular culture, in which absurdist violence plays such a large part. In doing so, they offered powerful confirmation of theorizing in film studies on this very question (Gormley 2005; King 2009; Paul 1994).

There are various competencies involved in "thinking like." Among these are "thinking unlike"—bringing a tangential or nondisciplinary perspective to the norms and prejudices of a discipline. Many of the most paradigm-shattering discoveries in the hard sciences and the most transformative theories in the soft sciences have arisen because of this tangential status. During the mid-1990s, I taught courses in African American literature to classes composed overwhelmingly of African American students. As a white male, my standing was that of an outsider. My students and I found that this status encouraged a closer look at many assumptions about black culture that would otherwise have gone unquestioned. Let your students guide you toward some of the big unasked questions in your field.

Accept Student Discomfort. Society at large and the marketing decisions of higher education institutions have schooled students to expect consumer service and certification over investigation and intellectual self-discovery (Graff 2003; McDonough 1997; Newfield 2008; Pope 2003). This informal schooling that students receive is in direct contrast to the various points in this checklist that I have offered. Each point in this checklist involves a degree of anxious self-consciousness about advanced intellectual activity on the part of students. Such strategies of engagement cross long-established boundaries between the institution of education and the self. This uncomfortableness must be honored, and then usefully folded back into learning; discomfort made manifest is an important early step in disengaging from rote practices. Because it is a novel classroom experience that reveals the self, ego-involved learning should be uncomfortable. In cinema studies, I'm often confronted by categorical resistance on the part of my students; the film in question is too old, too foreign, too black-and-white, or just *too hard*. The genuinely new can be difficult and has the potential to defamiliarize and then make exciting what has been seen but never reflected on.

Aim for Relevance, Not Intellectual Ease. Nothing in what I've written encourages or even excuses either dumbing down, in content or presentation, the ideas of a college course or helplessly resorting to constant stimulation or freedom from serious criticism (Svensson and Wood 2007). Aiming for the surface accessibility of the subject material is not the point. Quite the reverse: with enough attention to individual needs, I'm convinced that there is no set of ideas that is "too hard" for even an ordinary college student intellect. I have too often seen a student visibly thrilled by her ownership of serious, complex ideas to believe in the congenital idiocy of the American college student.

Transforming Entitlement into Engagement

Faculty and students now have a historic opportunity to honestly engage our mutual entitlements, and thus to vitalize American higher education. Transformations are occurring in every corner of higher education, technically, economically, philosophically, politically, and certainly in the psychology of the student. Those transformations will happen whether we guide them or not. If we choose not to guide them, many of the most nihilistic student behaviors that spring from this entitlement will only grow in dysfunctional effect (Blum 2009).

What results from our best efforts can truly entitle individual students, not merely with a diploma, but with selfhood, with independence, with generosity, with intellectual creativity, and with the courage and skill to use these entitlements to benefit themselves at the same moment they benefit the world. And we need those benefits immediately, for we are citizens first and professors second. Like our students, we can no longer afford to be comfortable with college only as a certification ritual or as a social event that extends adolescence for four years. We are not entitled to that.

References

Bain, K. 2004. *What the Best College Teachers Do.* Cambridge, MA: Harvard University Press.
Becker, W. E. 2000. "Teaching Economics in the 21st Century." *Journal of Economic Perspectives* 14 (1): 109–119.
Benveniste, G. 1977. *Bureaucracy.* San Francisco: Boyd & Fraser.
Berube, M. 2006. *What's Liberal about the Liberal Arts? Classroom Politics and "Bias" in Higher Education.* New York: W.W. Norton.

Blum, S. D. 2009. *My Word! Plagiarism and College Culture*. Ithaca, NY: Cornell University Press.

Booth, A. 2003. *Teaching History at University: Enhancing Learning and Understanding*. New York: Routledge.

Bruffee, K. 1999. *Collaborative Learning: Higher Education, Interdependence, and the Authority of Knowledge*, 2nd ed. Baltimore: Johns Hopkins University Press.

Cox, R. 2009. *The College Fear Factor: How Students and Professors Misunderstand One Another*. Cambridge, MA: Harvard University Press.

Currie, R. 2004. *Animal Houses: Fraternities in Film, 1978–2003*. Honor's thesis, Pennsylvania State University.

Elavsky, M., C. Mislan, and S. Elavsky. 2011. "When Talking Less Is More: Exploring Outcomes of Twitter Usage in the Large-Lecture Hall." *Learning, Media, and Technology* 36 (3): 215–233.

Fass, P. 1977. *The Damned and the Beautiful: American Youth in the 1920's*. New York: Oxford University Press.

Frank, T., and M. Weiland, eds. 1997. *Commodify Your Dissent: Salvos from the Baffler*. New York: W.W. Norton.

Gallagher, B. 2008. *Swimming in the Current: Six Essays on the Teachings of Writing Here and Now*. Unpublished manuscript.

Geisler, C. 1994. *Academic Literacy and the Nature of Expertise: Reading, Writing, and Knowing in Academic Philosophy*. Mahwah, NJ: Erlbaum.

Gordon, L., and L. Sahagun. 2007. "Gen Y's Ego Trip Takes a Bad Turn: A New Report Suggests That an Overdose of Self-Esteem in College Students Could Mean a Rough Road Ahead." *Los Angeles Times*, February 27, B1.

Gormley, P. 2005. *The New-Brutality Film: Race and Affect in Contemporary Hollywood Cinema*. Bristol, UK: Intellect.

Gottlieb, L. 2011. "How the Cult of Self-Esteem Is Ruining Our Kids." *The Atlantic* 2011 (July/August): 64–78.

Graff, G. 2003. *Clueless in Academe: How Schooling Obscures the Life of the Mind*. New Haven, CT: Yale University Press.

Hacker, A., and C. Dreifus. 2010. *Higher Education?* New York: Times Books.

Hedges, C. 2009. *Empire of Illusion: The End of Literacy and the Triumph of Spectacle*. New York: Nation Books.

Illich, I. 1983. *Deschooling Society*. New York: Harper & Row.

Keniston, K. 1965. "Social Change and Youth in America." In *The Challenge of Youth*, edited by E. H. Erikson, 191–222. Garden City, NY: Doubleday.

King, M. 2009. *The American Cinema of Excess: Extremes of the National Mind on Film*. Jefferson, NC: McFarland.

Krueger, J. I., K. D. Vohs, and R. F. Baumeister. 2008. "Is the Allure of Self-Esteem a Mirage After All?" *American Psychologist* 63 (1): 64–65.

McConachie, S. M., and A. R. Petrosky. 2010. "Disciplinary Literacy: A Principle-Based Framework." In *Content Matters: A Disciplinary Approach to Improving Student Learning*, edited by S. M. McConachie and A. R. Petrosky, 15–32. San Francisco: Jossey-Bass.

McDonough, P. 1997. *Choosing Colleges: How Social Class and Schools Structure Inequality*. Albany: State University of New York Press.

Menand, L. 2010. *The Marketplace of Ideas: Reform and Resistance in the American University*. New York: W.W. Norton.

Moffat, M. 1989. *Coming of Age in New Jersey: College and American Culture*. New Brunswick, NJ: Rutgers University Press.

Nelson, C., ed. 1986. *Theory in the Classroom*. Urbana: University of Illinois Press.

Newfield, C. 2008. *Unmaking the Public University: The Forty Year Assault on the Middle Class*. Cambridge, MA: Harvard University Press.

Paul, W. 1994. *Laughing, Screaming: Modern Hollywood Horror and Comedy*. New York: Columbia University Press.

Pope, D. C. 2003. *Doing School: How We Are Creating a Generation of Stressed-Out, Materialistic, and Miseducated Students*. New Haven, CT: Yale University Press.

Ramsden, P. 1992. *Learning to Teach in Higher Education*. New York: Routledge.

Rucin, S. (producer), and D. Fincher (director). 2010. *The Social Network* [motion picture]. Culver City, CA: Columbia Pictures.

Selber, S. 2004. *Multiliteracies for a Digital Age*. Carbondale: Southern Illinois University Press.

Seyforth, S. C., and C. M. Golde. 2001. "Beyond the Paper Chase: Using Movies to Help Students Get More out of College." *About Campus* 6 (4): 1–32.

Sperber, M. 2000. *Beer and Circus: How Big Time College Sports Is Crippling Undergraduate Education*. New York: Henry Holt.

Svensson, G., and G. Wood. 2007. "Are University Students Really Customers? When Illusion May Lead to Delusion for All!" *International Journal of Educational Management* 21 (1): 17–28.

Turkle, S. 2011. *Alone Together: Why We Expect More from Technology and Less from Each Other*. New York: Basic Books.

Twenge, J. M., and W. K. Campbell. 2009. *The Narcissism Epidemic: Living in an Age of Entitlement*. New York: Free Press.

Wolfe, T. 2004. *I Am Charlotte Simmons*. New York: Farrar, Straus & Giroux.

KEVIN JACK HAGOPIAN *teaches cinema studies and media studies at the Pennsylvania State University. While teaching at the University of Memphis, he was the first winner of the University's distinguished teaching award.*

NEW DIRECTIONS FOR TEACHING AND LEARNING • DOI: 10.1002/tl

2

If professors are to appropriately affirm Millennial students' egos, then those professors must understand the distinctions between ego entitlement and ego engagement.

Navigating the Paradox of Student Ego

Dave S. Knowlton

At one time or another, most professors probably have claimed that Millennial students' egos get in the way of learning. This claim is partially true. While *ego entitlement* can thwart learning, *ego engagement* can motivate and propel students to new heights that enhance learning. This chapter explicates these two aspects of student ego, and then points out some ways that professors unknowingly may perpetuate ego entitlement while hindering ego engagement. The last section of the chapter presents guidelines for enhancing students' ego engagement.

Ego Entitlement as Closed Aloofness

When discussing students' ego entitlements, faculty members often use synonyms of arrogance, presumptuousness, and self-centeredness. Such synonyms may not be completely baseless, but professors must have a more nuanced understanding of ego entitlement if they are to help students move beyond their own entitlements. Such nuance involves both a definition of ego entitlement and consideration of its causes.

Behavioral and Psychological Definitions. The behavioral facets of ego entitlement might be most familiar to faculty members, but the psychological aspects provide more fundamental insights into the ways that ego can hinder learning and create an unproductive sense of entitlement.

Behavioral. Ego entitlement often is displayed through violations of a social contract as defined by course syllabi, institutional policies, and academic traditions. Sometimes these violations show up in ways that seem

NEW DIRECTIONS FOR TEACHING AND LEARNING, no. 135, Fall 2013 © Wiley Periodicals, Inc.
Published online in Wiley Online Library (wileyonlinelibrary.com) • DOI: 10.1002/tl.20060

to be caricatures of aloofness. For example, one student told me that tardiness was beyond her control. Why? Her mother was "always late for everything." When I pointed out to her that she was just blaming her tardiness on genetics, she neither acquiesced nor retreated. As an even more dramatic caricature, one of my colleagues tells a story of receiving an e-mail from a student at 11:50 p.m. The e-mail contained an assignment that was due by midnight. Other e-mails from the same student arrived at 11:56 p.m., 11:58 p.m., and 12:04 a.m.; each of those subsequent e-mails was criticizing the professor for having not yet acknowledged the assignment submission.

Ego entitlement seems particularly defiant in areas related to course grades. For example, students have been known to express contempt toward an earned grade because they needed a higher grade point average in order to keep a scholarship or enter graduate school (Ciani, Summers, and Easter 2008). Furthermore, many students claim the right to higher grades when they define their own efforts as strong, even if achievement does not accompany those efforts (Adams 2005). The mainstream press even has reported examples of ego entitlements related to grading practices: "A recent study ... found that a third of students surveyed said that they expected Bs just for attending lectures, and 40 percent said they deserved a B for completing the required reading" (Roosevelt 2009, A15). These student expressions seem to indicate disrespect toward professors, courses, learning, and the enterprise of academia.

Psychological. Ego entitlement has dimensions beyond students' hackneyed behaviors; ego entitlement is psychological. Perhaps, for example, understanding ego entitlement requires consideration of students' emotional health. After all, only 52 percent of college freshmen report their emotional health as being "above average"; the rest of them report large waves of being "depressed, stressed and [overly] anxious" (Fendrich 2011, para. 2). I am not qualified to make arguments about the status of students' emotional health. I am, however, equipped to frame the psychological construct of ego entitlement as it relates to educational interactions. The construction that follows is not definitive; instead, it serves as one way to explicate students' psyche of entitlement. In what follows, I conceptualize ego entitlement in terms of the value of being "closed" to others, to ideas, and to the self. By adopting this three-pronged stance of being closed, Millennial students promote the intrapersonal protections of psychological safety and risk adversity. Such protections allay their depression, stress, and anxiousness.

Millennial students often seem to be closed to others. For example, relative to their counterparts from earlier generations, Millennial students have a low sense of empathy (Konrath, O'Brien, and Hsing 2011). A lack of empathy certainly would lead to interpersonal instability and negative outcomes regarding relationships, both of which are correlated with ego entitlement (Campbell et al. 2004). Cumulatively, these characteristics of ego

NEW DIRECTIONS FOR TEACHING AND LEARNING • DOI: 10.1002/tl

entitlement are "robust, distinctive predictor(s)" of right-fighting and blaming (Exline et al. 2004, 909).

The remaining two prongs—being closed to ideas and being closed to the self—can be illustrated through a single anecdote: Several semesters ago, I used the first day of class to explain the guidelines for a variety of assignments that were designed to help students connect course content with their own beliefs, values, and experiences. As one student was leaving the room, he said, "Okay, Dave, I'll do all these personal writings and synthesis assignments, but I'm certain that I won't learn anything from doing them." This student illustrated that he was closed both to allowing the content to pierce his ego circle and to embracing course content as a meaningful tool for personal rejuvenation. Being closed in this way is not necessarily unusual, as many college students equate meaningful learning with memorizing information and remembering facts (Cox 2009).

Why are many students closed to content and the potential power inherent to substantive ideas? Broudy (1994) offers a viable explanation: Ideas that truly are engaging and meaningful must contain "[t]ension, suspense, and drama," all of which require an embracing of nonconformity and risk. Nonconformity and risk compromise feelings of personal security; by staying away from engaging and meaningful ideas, then, students can "reduce fear and anxiety" (Broudy 1994, 9). But, by aiming for safety and conformity, students often end up in a pure state of intellectual inertness (Csikszentmihalyi 2008).

On the surface, we perceive college students as being open only to themselves, their own existences, and their own needs—"I couldn't be in class yesterday; did I miss anything?" Upon closer examination, that openness is, at best, superficial. That is, the state of intellectual inertness that comes from being closed to ideas is heightened because students sometimes are closed to the self. A lot of them are "out of touch with ... why they are even in college" (Hassel and Lourey 2005, 2); passion, joy, and personal purpose seem to have eluded many Millennial students. The feeling of not knowing why they are in college can lead to the idea that they are not worthy of being in college; thus, they do not allow themselves to enjoy the experience of learning.

This type of being closed to the self is a state of "creative withdrawal" (Cameron 1992, 6) that metaphorically can reduce one to "sitting there panting like a lapdog" or "unintentionally making slow asthmatic death rattles" (Lamott 1995, 17–18). More literally, students who are closed to themselves are unable to direct their own consciousness and reflect on those self-directions (Csikszentmihalyi 2008). Much of what professors ask of them, then, seems like some kind of insult because they do not see the potential dividends of investing themselves. Students remedy their own myopia by approaching learning tasks in perfunctory ways and acting out in defense of their own sense of fundamentally being entitled to something more.

Causes and Influences of Ego Entitlement. At its broadest, ego entitlement may well be a by-product of contemporary American society. I certainly am not the first to make such an allegation, as Dyer (2006, 157) notes that we are "fully immersed" in a society where most people were raised "to believe in the illusion of ego [entitlement]." Because of this belief, society has "develop[ed] and evolve[d] firmly committed to a false self" (157). For example, dominant powers within the United States have indoctrinated students into accepting a conventional, narrow, and inappropriate view of education. This indoctrination begins during students' precollege education, and it sets the tone for entitled behaviors and a psychological state of being closed.

Broudy (1994) notes that inappropriate values, attitudes, and norms result in "joyless ... obligation" to complete tasks not because of their meaningfulness but because there is a "general expectation" that those tasks "will be carried out" (6–7). Consider that a preponderance of students' precollege education is based on impersonal rituals of memorizing and regurgitating. Through the repetition of this ritual, students have been conditioned toward completing mundane tasks mindlessly, not challenged and inspired to become absorbed in rich and engaging opportunities that better lead to enlightenment and meaningful learning.

This conditioning is reinforced by an often-repeated mantra that many students hear regularly throughout their precollege education: "Just make good grades, and you can write your own ticket." We should not be surprised, then, when students are enraptured with a motivation to earn the prize of a high grade in order to improve their lot in life. And because of conventional wisdom, many students never consider that the connections between the prize and an improved life may well be suspect.

The conditioning and convention often influence students' attitudes toward higher education (Hassel and Lourey 2005). As Herbert (2011, para. 5) says, "Perhaps more now than ever, the point of the college experience is to have a good time and walk away with a valuable credential after putting in the least effort possible." Indeed, contemporary American education has taught many students that getting their "voucher punched" serves as commodity and capital that take precedence over learning, self-development, and enlightenment. As one university junior said to me, "I define myself by my GPA."

Ego Engagement as Opened Allowing

This chapter has painted a depressing picture so far. If, however, we consider the possibility that an alternative conception of ego exists and if we further accept that this alternative provides opportunity for redressing ego entitlement, then optimism can prevail. Contrasting ego entitlement is the possibility for students to achieve ego engagement. At its broadest, we might equate ego engagement with "peak experience" (Maslow 1976), "artistic recovering" (Cameron 1992), an "expansive tendency" (Csikszent-mihalyi 1996), "intention" (Dyer 2004), "spirit" (Dyer 2006), or "flow" (Csikszentmihalyi 2008). These conceptualizations, on the one hand, all are uniquely detailed, each requiring a book-length manuscript for explication; yet, on the other hand, they each are ethereal, elusive, and ineffable. In fact, any explanation of ego engagement in a "sober, cool, analytic, 'scientific' way succeeds only with those who already know what you mean"— those who can "feel or intuit what you are trying to point to even when your words are quite inadequate in themselves" (Maslow 1976, 84). To summarize the point: Because of both the depth and ethereality of ego engagement, defining it coherently and succinctly is difficult. At the risk of oversimplification, this section frames ego engagement as a state of being and a process.

State of Being. Ego engagement contrasts with ego entitlement. If ego entitlement is routine, conventional, joyless, and intellectually inert, all of which are manifestations of being closed and promoting psychological safety, then ego engagement is spontaneous, innovative, blissful, and forward thinking, all of which are a result of openly and vulnerably embracing bold intellectual exploration. This definition of opposites has bolstering from business guru Stephen Covey (2006), who encourages Millennial students to be "humble" and open to new experiences that promote "high learning curve(s)" (56).

Within this state of ego engagement, a loss of self-consciousness allows students to become "part of a system of action greater than what the individual self had been before" (Csikszentmihalyi 2008, 65). For the ego-engaged student, a symbiotic relationship exists among the self, course content, and positive energies that engage the intellectual (Csikszentmihalyi 2008), spiritual (Dyer 2006), aesthetic (Broudy 1994), and emotional (Cameron 1992) sensibilities. This symbiosis results in an intimate and complex connection between "the genuine needs of the self" and one's "concrete environment" (Csikszentmihalyi 2008, 20).

Process. The described state of being does not magically and spontaneously erupt. For Millennial students to achieve that state, they must engage in processes that reside just beyond the border of routine and convention and within a land of productive anxiety (Csikszentmihalyi 2008). Perhaps these processes involve models with identifiable phases or steps. For instance, crystalized processes of creating (see, for example, Cameron 1992) or designing (see, for example, Gabriel-Petit 2010) could allow for ego engagement. Csikszentmihalyi (2008) points to the steps of setting goals, receiving feedback, focusing concentration, and modifying goals as a process of finding a genuine sense of ego engagement.

The underlying structure of rational algorithms and fruitful heuristics might be relevant, but a process-based definition of ego engagement must embrace forces that transcend those structures. As Wang (2010) suggests, an "imaginative intuition of knowledge" often is more relevant to learning than is either empiricism or rationalism (176). Similarly, Csikszentmihalyi (1996) notes that meaningful idea incubation occurs in the subconscious, below the level of identifiable rationalism.

More provocatively, we also must accept the mystical influence of inspiration. Inspiration is a process in which "an idea has taken hold of us from the invisible reality of spirit." When we experience inspiration, "we allow ourselves to be moved by a force that's more powerful than our ego [entitlement] and all of its illusions" (Dyer 2006, 6). If Dyer is right, then to reject inspiration is to disconnect from ego-engaged learning. To fully embrace inspiration, learners must vigorously engage themselves in meaningful tasks; but they also must succumb to the notion that learning sometimes cannot be controlled or forced. It only can be allowed. Through this process of allowing, ego-engaged students are effected and become open to a central question as asked by Holmes (1996, 24): "What will all this [education] do to me?" This question is important; by asking it, students affirm a true desire to embody the full irony of ego engagement: Ego engagement requires "ego surrender" that will lead students to discover "a new sense of self marked by increased autonomy, resilience, expectancy, and excitement—as well as by the capacity to make and execute concrete creative plans" (Cameron 1992, 5–6).

Do Professors Have Ownership in Perpetuating Ego Entitlement?

Faculty members unknowingly might perpetuate ego entitlement through their own assumptions about students. Consider that "[t]oday's youth seem to be no more egotistical than previous generations." In fact, they "seem to have psychological profiles that are remarkably similar to youth from the past 30 years" (Trzesniewski and Donnellan 2010, 69–70). So, on the one hand, faculty members perceive ego entitlement as real and problematic; on the other hand, some evidence suggests that ego entitlement may not exist. This contradiction can be explained in terms of perspective: "When we complain about [generational] values ... and are challenged to give reasons for our disapproval, we point to the violation of some norm we consider valid" (Broudy 1994, 7). Arnett (2010) seems to affirm the importance of the words "we consider valid" by noting that older generations may be tempted to apply inappropriate and outdated norms when judging Millennial students. In sum, ego entitlements of Millennial students might exist only through the lens of professors from a previous generation.

Professors perpetuate ego entitlement in more active ways, too. For instance, some evidence suggests that students and professors are "partners" in promoting ego entitlement (Boice 2000, 84). Professors sometimes respond to student incivility, disrespect, and disengagement in ways that make them seem distant and disinterested (Plax and Kearney 1992).

NEW DIRECTIONS FOR TEACHING AND LEARNING • DOI: 10.1002/tl

Distance and disinterest might imply that professors do not take students' ideas seriously (Lewin 2011). The students, then, feel slighted and may respond with additional uncivil and disrespectful behaviors (Boice 2000). The result is a spiral of unproductive interaction that is contributed to by both professors and students. Because professors are the formal authority in the classroom, they must accept ownership of this unproductive spiral.

Perhaps some professors even reinforce ego entitlement through pedagogy. Many professors still promote the myth that to learn is to memorize. Because content to be memorized must be more factual, that content lacks the types of suspense, tension, and drama that allow students to become ego-engaged learners. At its core, a pedagogy based on memorization implicitly embraces the metaphor of "filling students" with knowledge. When students accept this metaphor and their implied role of serving as a passive receptacle and intellectual concubine, they also are accepting the improbability of experiencing flow, openness, inspiration, and other elements of learning that typify ego engagement. Furthermore, the metaphor of "filling" implies a parallel of students "emptying themselves" as a show of achievement. This parallel metaphor belies ego engagement and provides students with an excuse to remain interpersonally and intrapersonally closed.

Earlier in this chapter, as I described students' psychological state of being closed, I suggested that they do not allow themselves to enjoy the experience of learning. This conclusion is quite exculpatory in blaming students for a shortcoming that may well belong to professors. Have professors taught students *how* to enjoy the experience? Classrooms are unique and idiosyncratic, each providing students with different opportunities for genuine joy, pleasures, and breathtaking moments. Professors, then, have an obligation to educate students through processes that not only advance learning but also foster enjoyment. Certainly, if professors only engage students in impersonal processes of being filled and emptied, then opportunities for joy, inspiration, and happiness that are the cornerstone of ego-engaged learning give way to monotony and disengagement.

Even faculty members who promote more substantive types of learning often retain rules that hinder ego-engaged experiences. For example, many faculty members emphasize rational and dualistic thought that is grounded in empiricism. Cameron (1992) labels this positivist empirical ontology as privileging "logic brain"—categorical, linear, and well structured (12–13). Such modes of thinking force students to defer to depersonalized conceptual structures and external measures of success. Learning can only be seen, then, as impersonal processes rooted in well-defined technique—the antithesis of connection, inspiration, and allowing. When faculty members promote absolute answers, strictly defined processes, and narrow parameters of acceptable technique, students view themselves as either "right" or "wrong." Students feel a need to right-fight for the former.

NEW DIRECTIONS FOR TEACHING AND LEARNING • DOI: 10.1002/tl

Guidelines for Leveraging Student Ego in the Classroom

A central premise of this volume is that professors must leverage student ego so that opportunities for ego engagement are more predominant than are chances for students to act on their sense of entitlement. My intention in the remainder of this chapter is to provide a framework for shaping students' mental models of *themselves* as ego-engaged learners. This shaping can occur by adapting a truth that I borrow from the world of the performing arts: It is possible to work on a student's psychology from the outside in.

Professors promote futility when they ask Millennial students to become more ego-engaged learners in an organic way. Such a request is purely hypothetical for two reasons. First, many students never have experienced the types of flow, openness, and inspiration that characterize ego-engaged learning; therefore, they cannot conceptualize ego engagement as a goal. Second, Millennial students cannot remake themselves into ego-engaged learners because many of them do not see anything wrong with their current understandings of their higher education learning experiences. The rest of this chapter delineates principles for shaping students' psychological views of their own potential for ego-engaged learning.

Promote Students as the Source of Ego-Engaged Learning. For several years now, I have started each semester by sharing with students a passage from Dyer (2006, 232):

> You may have never thought of yourself as a person who has genius residing within. You may have thought that genius is a word reserved for the Mozarts, Michelangelos, Einsteins, Madame Curies, Virginia Woolfs, Stephen Hawkings, and others whose lives and accomplishments have been publicized. But keep in mind that they share the same essence of consciousness that you do. ... [Therefore, genius is] available to every single human being. ... The qualities of creativity and genius are within you, waiting your decision to [express them].

Students often are a bit disconcerted by Dyer's language; but, through various discussions and activities, I attempt to help them discover the value of trusting their own ideas and beliefs. I let them know that I believe in the creative and intellectual power that lives within them; to access that power in productive ways, so my argument goes, they must come to believe in and trust it, too.

In some ways, sharing Dyer (2006) begins a cursory process of simply convincing students—not to mention reminding myself—that they are capable of achieving at high levels. The communication of such optimism is a critical component of setting a tone for meaningful learning (Cox 2009). More centrally, though, Dyer's quote provides an anchor for Bain's (2004) view that students must "begin struggling with [a content-based] issue from their own perspective" and "articulate a position" (110). I use Dyer's quote as support for the reasonableness of implementing Bain's approach.

Though they are not content experts, students do possess a sense of genius that must be harnessed toward the goal of developing their "artist brain." Such a brain experiences learning through creative shadings and "freewheeling" associations (Cameron 1992, 13). Csikszentmihalyi (1996) likely would agree; he argues the need to focus on the lived experience of people by placing *their* ideas, problems, and discoveries at the center of activity. Making content the center, Csikszentmihalyi points out, is more likely to stifle the very types of achievement that could result in ego-engaged learning.

Broaden Habits of Mind Beyond Comfort Zones. If the processes of ego engagement are to succeed, then students must be stretched beyond their cognitive, psychological, and emotional comfort zones. Playing it safe and remaining entrenched in comfort will not be transactional enough to obtain a state of ego engagement. One way to broaden students' habits of mind is to immerse them in authentic contexts so that they can participate in real-world problem solving. Fidelity to beyond-classroom contexts is preferable to traditional course assignments (Bain 2004; Gabriel-Petit 2010; Wang 2010). Still, *doing* is not enough to engage ego; after all, people do real-world tasks every day, yet many are surprisingly unreflective about—and unchanged by—those tasks.

I agree with Hassel and Lourey (2005) that we must "teach students not only the content of our disciplines but also the habits of mind that will help them learn the conventions of college life, study effectively and purposefully, and succeed in their chosen fields" (3). Opportunities abound for emphasizing a variety of thinking approaches, all of which will broaden habits of mind: visual thinking (Arnheim 1969), critical thinking (Brookfield, 1987), socially relevant thinking (Wang 2010), reflective thinking (Knowlton, 2010), and creative thinking (Csikszentmihalyi 1996), which in itself might depend on divergent, imaginative, receptive, transformative, and evaluative thinking (Carson 2010). In activating this wide variety of thinking approaches, professors ought to insist upon interactions that require students to think in ways that they are neither inclined toward nor comfortable with. In so doing, professors can support true ego engagement.

Focus on the Spiritual. Covey (2006) points to "the key," which is to "inspire" Millennial college students "to find their unique talent and passion ... so that their security comes from within" (56). Finding one's personal talents and passions requires a spiritual focus (Dyer 2006; Holmes 1996; Murphy 2005). Elsewhere, I phrased it this way:

> If finding one's own substance and passion is inherently spiritual and if find-
> ing substance and passions is inherently related to learning, then a

conclusion is clear: To not provide room for spiritual rumination within the classroom is to hinder learning. (Knowlton 2010, 77)

I am not advocating the overt integration of religious beliefs into secular classrooms; religion and spirituality are not the same (Bento 2000), as spirituality can be based in "naturalistic meaning" (Maslow 1976, 4). In order for students to experience both the state of being and processes that are inherent to ego-engaged learning, though, faculty members must prompt students to consider their own "inner experiences" and not be limited "to the tangible, the visible, the audible, [or] to that which can be recorded by a machine" (Maslow 1976, 6). Maslow's perspective is similar to Csikszentmihalyi's (2008) view that the "lack of inner order manifests itself in the subjective conditions [of] ontological anxiety or existential dread." This anxiety and dread creates a "fear of being" (12). As a result, students likely will not be able to achieve ego-engaged learning unless they confront the internal and subjective elements of the self that led to anxiety and dread. By providing students with an opportunity to deal with this sense of anxiety and dread, it is my belief that learning can become a cathartic experience that leads to unbridled joy, where students look within to reclaim experience and "harvest the genuine rewards of living" (Csikszentmihalyi 2008, 19).

Conclusion

This chapter might rightly lead faculty members to realize that Millennial students' egos are complex and paradoxical. In fact, faculty members should worry less about students being self-absorbed through entitlements and more about the possibility that students are not self-absorbed enough to become ego engaged in ways that meaningfully transcend the commonplace. Facilitating students' capacities and propensities to become ego engaged is hard work for serious scholars. If professors are to make significant contributions to the way that students understand both themselves and the potential of their own egos as a point of engaged learning, then they must spend substantive effort and time in interacting with students' mental models of self and learning. As ego-engaged professors, we must accept and act upon the belief that we can make a difference in the lives of students.

References

Adams, J. B. 2005. "What Makes the Grade? Faculty and Student Perceptions." *Teaching of Psychology* 32 (1): 21–24.

Arnett, J. J. 2010. "Oh, Grow Up! Generational Grumbling and the New Life Stage of Emerging Adulthood—Commentary on Trzesniewski & Donnellan (2010)." *Perspectives on Psychological Science* 5 (1): 89–92.

Arnheim, R. 1969. *Visual Thinking.* Berkeley: University of California Press.

Bain, K. 2004. *What the Best College Teachers Do.* Cambridge, MA: Harvard University Press.

Bento, R. F. 2000. "The Little Inn at the Crossroads: A Spiritual Approach to the Design of a Leadership Course." *Journal of Management Education* 24 (3): 650–661.

Boice, R. 2000. *Advice for New Faculty Members: Nihil Nimus.* Boston: Allyn & Bacon.

Brookfield, S. D. 1987. *Developing Critical Thinkers: Challenging Adults to Explore Alternative Ways of Thinking and Acting.* San Francisco: Jossey-Bass.

Broudy, H. S. 1994. *Enlightened Cherishing: An Essay on Aesthetic Education.* Urbana: University of Illinois Press.

Cameron, J. 1992. *The Artist's Way: A Spiritual Path to Higher Creativity.* New York: Penguin Putnam.

Campbell, W., A. M. Bonacci, J. Shelton, J. J. Exline, and B. J. Bushman. 2004. "Psychological Entitlement: Consequences and Validations of a Self-Report Measure." *Journal of Personality Assessment* 83 (1): 29–45.

Carson, S. 2010. *Your Creative Brain: Seven Steps to Maximize Imagination, Productivity, and Innovation in Your Life.* San Francisco: Jossey-Bass.

Ciani, K. D., J. J. Summers, and M. A. Easter. 2008. "Gender Differences in Academic Entitlement among College Students." *Journal of Genetic Psychology* 169 (4): 332–344.

Covey, S. 2006. "Questions for Covey: Redefining HR's Role for Success." *Training Magazine* 10: 56.

Cox, R. D. 2009. *The College Fear Factor: How Students and Professors Misunderstand One Another.* Cambridge, MA: Harvard University Press.

Csikszentmihalyi, M. 1996. *Creativity: Flow and the Psychology of Discovery and Invention.* New York: Harper Perennial.

Csikszentmihalyi, M. 2008. *Flow: The Psychology of Optimal Experience.* New York: Harper Perennial.

Dyer, W. 2004. *The Power of Intention: Learning to Cocreate Your World Your Way.* Carlsbad, CA: Hay House.

Dyer, W. 2006. *Inspiration: Your Ultimate Calling.* Carlsbad, CA: Hay House.

Exline, J. J., R. F. Baumeister, B. J. Bushman, W. K. Campbell, and E. J. Finkel. 2004. "Too Proud to Let Go: Narcissistic Entitlement as a Barrier to Forgiveness." *Journal of Personality and Social Psychology* 87 (6): 894–912.

Fendrich, L. 2011. "College Freshmen and Their Postmodern Dread." *Chronicle of Higher Education*, January 27. Accessed February 7, 2011. http://chronicle .com/blogs/brainstorm/college-freshmen-and-their-postmodern-dread/31560.

Gabriel-Petit, P. 2010. "Design Is a Process, Not a Methodology." *UXMatters*, July 19. http://www.uxmatters.com/mt/archives/2010/07/design-is-a-process-not-a -methodology.php.

Hassel, H., and J. Lourey. 2005. "The Dea(r)th of Student Responsibility." *College Teaching* 53 (1): 2–13.

Herbert, B. 2011. "College the Easy Way." *New York Times*, March 4, A21. http://www .nytimes.com/2011/03/05/opinion/05herbert.html.

Holmes, A. 1996. *The Idea of a Christian College*, rev. ed. Grand Rapids, MI: Eerdmans.

Knowlton, D. S. 2010. "Take Out the Tests, and Hide the Grades; Add the Spiritual with All Voices Raised! Professor Explications and Students' Opinions of an Unconventional Classroom Milieu." *Critical Questions in Education* 1 (2): 70–93.

Konrath, S., E. H. O'Brien, and C. Hsing. 2011. "Changes in Dispositional Empathy in American College Students over Time: A Meta-Analysis." *Personality and Social Psychological Review* 15 (2): 180–198.

Lamott, A. 1995. *Bird by Bird: Some Instructions on Writing and Life.* New York: Anchor Books.

Lewin, T. 2011. "Record Level of Stress Found in College Freshmen." *New York Times*, January 27, A1. http://www.nytimes.com/2011/01/27/education/27colleges.html?_r= 1&scp=1&sq=education%20stress%20college%20students&st=cse.

Maslow, A. H. 1976. *Religions, Values, and Peak-Experiences.* New York: Penguin Books.

Murphy, C. 2005. "The Academy, Spirituality, and the Search for Truth." In *Spirituality in Higher Education*, edited by S. L. Hoppe and B. W. Speck, 23–29. San Francisco: Jossey-Bass.

Plax, T. G., and P. K. Kearney. 1992. "Teacher Power in the Classroom." In *Power in the Classroom*, edited by V. P. Richmond and J. C. McCroskey, 67–84. Hillsdale, NJ: Erlbaum.

Roosevelt, M. 2009. "Student Expectations Seen as Causing Grade Disputes." *New York Times*, February 18, A15. http://www.nytimes.com/2009/02/18/education/18college.html.

Trzesniewski, K. H., and M. B. Donnellan. 2010. "Rethinking 'Generation Me': A Study of Cohort Effects From 1976–2006." *Perspectives on Psychological Science* 5 (1): 58–75.

Wang, T. 2010. "A New Paradigm for Design Studio Education." *International Journal of Art & Design Education* 29 (2): 173–183.

DAVE S. KNOWLTON *is professor of instructional technology at Southern Illinois University Edwardsville.*

NEW DIRECTIONS FOR TEACHING AND LEARNING • DOI: 10.1002/tl

Data from a focus group of undergraduate students confirm that students view themselves as deserving entitled treatment in higher education.

3

What Students Say about Their Own Sense of Entitlement

Darren S. Fullerton

Headlines proclaim a greater sense of student entitlement than ever before: "New Data on College Students and Overconfidence" (Irvine 2011), "Teaching the Entitled Generation" (Miller 2009), "Student Expectations Seen as Causing Grade Disputes" (Roosevelt 2009), and the list goes on.

Because students are coming to campus with perspectives and egos that have been shaped by overindulgent parents, technology, social media, the Internet, and disposable income (Rhee, Sanders, and Simpson 2010), many experts contend that students believe they are entitled to, or deserving of, professors providing them with certain treatments, services, and benefits (Howe and Strauss 2007). What's more concerning is that these perks seem unrelated to students' actual performance responsibilities inside the classroom (Singleton-Jackson, Jackson, and Reinhardt 2010). This chapter presents students' perspectives about issues surrounding their sense of entitlement.

Focus Group Participants and Format

Sixty-seven students from three first-year university experience seminars were randomly selected for participation in focus groups about the attitudes and expectations of college students. Participants included 31 females and 36 males. The students completed a student-viewpoint questionnaire consisting of 25 questions and signed up for prearranged focus group sessions. Each of the questions was discussed during the focus group sessions.

New Directions for Teaching and Learning, no. 135, Fall 2013 © Wiley Periodicals, Inc.
Published online in Wiley Online Library (wileyonlinelibrary.com) • DOI: 10.1002/tl.20061

The essence of students' perceptions and observations encompassed the classroom environment, the role of the student, and the role of professors. Prior to addressing each of those aspects, however, this chapter examines a customer service mentality that seemed either implicitly assumed or explicitly stated during the focus groups.

Customer Service and Consumer Mentality

In response to the question of whether they "deserve to be treated as a customer of the university," the students gave a resounding "Yes." Only two students stated that they did not like the term *customer*. Those two preferred the term *consumer*, which implies the right to go elsewhere for better service. The majority of the students agreed that they "expect to get quality in service" because of the "high price" that they pay for college.

To examine student expectations as customers, the students were asked: "What do you deserve from the university in exchange for the money that you pay in tuition and fees?" Responses to this question included "a good education," "teachers who care about their students," and "assistance from my professors." To the agreement of many other participants, one student said, "With the high cost of tuition, I think that we should get free iPads. These would help us be better students."

The claim of being customers and consumers extended beyond items that might ensure learning and quality education; those claims rapidly seemed to encompass issues of individual and personal benefit. To this end, comments included items such as "not paying fees for things that do not pertain to me or that I did not ask for." Example items included fees for the recreation center, health center, and parking. Other students commented on the need for "better food in the residence halls" and "DirectTV instead of cable."

One issue vividly illustrates the customer mentality and encompasses classroom rules, the role of the student, and the role of the professor. Specifically, the issue related to e-mail. Seventy-eight percent of the students in the study indicated that it was the professor's duty to respond to their e-mail within 24 hours. In contrast, only 45 percent of these same students felt that they should respond to a professor's e-mail in this same 24-hour period. As one student said, "Professors should be held to a different standard. Professors should check their e-mail daily, but as students, sometimes we can only check it once a week." A discussion as to the reasons for this double standard led to an almost unanimous agreement with the comments that "faculty do this for a living [and] are getting paid. ... We (as students) are in several classes and have lives outside of the university. Faculty do not."

Classroom Environment, Rules, and Courtesy

Several issues surrounding the classroom environment and accompanying rules were discussed. One such issue was related to attendance and

NEW DIRECTIONS FOR TEACHING AND LEARNING • DOI: 10.1002/tl

tardiness. An overwhelming majority of participants indicated that since they were paying for their education, it should be their choice of whether to attend class, when to arrive, and when to leave. The only concern voiced regarding this subject was that if a student was leaving class early or arriving late, that student should do so without interrupting others in class.

The next issue discussed was the use of cell phones in class. Though the groups seemed to be evenly split on whether students should be allowed to answer their cell phones in class, only 10 percent indicated that a student should not answer the phone in class. Further discussion led 90 percent of the students to indicate that they felt students should be allowed to exit the class to answer the phone. On the subject of texting during class, 97 percent of the students strongly supported the perception that it is acceptable to text during class. One student said, "The professor might think that this is rude, but we are paying for the class." Another seemed to agree: "If that is how we choose to use our time, then that is what we should be allowed to do. We are paying for it."

Students took issue with policies surrounding late work. Nearly 100 percent of the students in the focus groups stated that the university should impose a standard policy that forces professors to accept late work from students. One student's comment struck a chord with the others when she stated, "We are paying for the class up front, and you are teaching it over the course of the semester. Why are we not given the assignments up front, and then given the opportunity to turn them in at any point in the semester?"

The Role of the Student

Students perceived their own role as having an end point of employment. The students unanimously indicated that their primary purpose was to get a degree in hopes of securing a better-paying job than the jobs available to high school graduates. To the agreement of many, one student indicated that "getting a job is the goal, and with that goal, how much time it takes to complete a degree is a huge issue."

A great deal of discussion focused on the students' perceptions of their role in getting an education versus getting training. Many students questioned the "liberal arts approach" to education. One student responded, "We do not have the interest (or the time) for many of the subjects that the university forces us to take." Many other students supported this perception with comments such as: "I am a business major. By requiring me take classes in areas like music, theater, literature, and so on, the university is just trying to make more money off students by requiring additional classes that are not needed for my chosen career field."

Ninety percent of the respondents agreed that students must exert effort to be successful. However, discussion regarding student responsibilities lacked a great deal of clarity. The students, as a whole, could not agree on what constitutes effort and how much of it is necessary. Certainly, students acknowledged that their role was to "show up for class," "be on time," "be respectful," "do the assignments," and "participate." These comments, though, appeared to be the conditioned response to standard questions. Upon simple probing, many of the students could not substantively define and illustrate the meaning of terms like *respect* and *participation*. "Being respectful," for example, was described as "showing up for class, sitting quietly/not disrupting class, and doing your assignments."

The Role of the Professor

"We are paying the instructor's salary," most students agreed, so they had much to say about the role of the professor in the classroom. Student views regarding the role of the professor mirrored those attributes that have already been established as characteristics of effective teaching, such as "being respectful, knowledgeable, approachable, engaging, communicative, organized, responsive, professional, and humorous" (Delaney et al. 2010, 25). Key items that students felt that they "deserved" from their professors focused on "clear expectations," "fair treatment," and "empathy for personal situations that might impact [student] classroom performance." To analyze this list, it is clear that students understand the role of the professor mostly in terms of their own needs and desires as customers.

What might be surprising is that students perceived a lack of faculty engagement with students. Most agreed that because they "pay huge amounts of money to be here and to get an education," professors should demonstrate that they "appreciate" their students. Beyond appreciation, students perceived professors to have low concern for students' welfare. Through a number of comments that were made with tones of deep conviction, students questioned the professors' concern, empathy, and support for each student.

Students also had much to say about professors' grading practices. When asked what grade they should be given for completing assigned readings and attending most class sessions, 44 percent stated that they deserved an A; 33 percent said that they deserved a B, with the rest indicating that they would most likely deserve a C. In an interesting contrast, when students were asked whether professors should consider student effort when assigning grades, their initial response was agreement with the student comment, "It is difficult to assess effort. I may be putting forth a great deal of effort, but I might not understand the material." Further discussion by the participants led most of the students to agree that effort must play an important role in assigning grades, even though 80 percent of the students were unable to articulate exactly how the professor was to assess their efforts.

As students were polled about the actual dynamics of assigning grades, 75 percent said that they did not expect the professor to "give" grades to students who were experiencing personal or medical issues outside of class. At odds with this statement was the perception that 90 percent of students indicated that it was appropriate for a professor to raise a student's grade that was one percentage point away from a higher grade.

Implications for the Classroom

Students arrive on our campuses expecting to have not only a voice but also a significant degree of control over that college experience (Singleton-Jackson, Jackson, and Reinhardt 2010). The results of these focus groups seem to support this perspective and suggest that students view themselves as customers who are paying for a consumer product. While many professors may question the usefulness of that metaphor, perhaps instead of objecting, it would be useful to embrace that metaphor in ways that help professors develop strategies for working with entitled students. Efforts to personalize the course experience for students, showing concern for their well-being both in class and outside of class, could assist in changing the students' attitudes about professorial engagement and therefore the quality of the learning experience that students are having.

In addition, an implication of students' perspectives is that professors should examine their policies, procedures, and practices. Where Millennial students are concerned, it may not be enough to have policies on attendance and cell phone usage. Instead, professors must help students understand the rationales for those policies. Can attendance requirements be connected directly to students developing necessary knowledge and skills that they might find meaningful? What is the rationale in telling students to turn off their smartphones instead of finding ways to incorporate smartphone tools in course activities? Even students' contradictions in the ways that they view grading may provide opportunities for professors to more deeply engage students in a process of examining their own learning. Many of our university colleagues comment about "meeting our students where they are." By considering students' voices and opinions, professors have a unique opportunity to productively "meet the students where they want to be."

References

Delaney, J. G., A. N. Johnson, T. D. Johnson, and D. L. Treslan. 2010. *Students' Perceptions of Effective Teaching in Higher Education.* St. John's, NL: Distance Education and Learning Technologies.

Howe, N., and W. Strauss. 2007. *Millennials Go to College,* 2nd ed. Great Falls, VA: LifeCourse Associates.

Irvine, M. 2011. "New Data on College Students and Overconfidence." *USA Today,* updated June 17. http://yourlife.usatoday.com/parenting-family/teen-ya/story/2011/06/Study-More-college-freshmen-feel-above-average/48498560/1.

Miller, K. 2009. "Teaching the Entitled Generation." *Converge Magazine,* July 14. Retrieved from http://www.convergemag.com/blog/whiteboard/Teaching-Entitled-Generation.html.

Rhee, C., G. L. Sanders, and N. C. Simpson. 2010. "I, Myself and e-Myself." *Communications of the ACM* 53: 154–157.

Roosevelt, M. 2009. "Student Expectations Seen as Causing Grade Disputes." *New York Times*, February 17. http://www.nytimes.com/2009/02/18/education/18college.html.

Singleton-Jackson, J., D. Jackson, and J. Reinhardt. 2010. "Students as Consumers of Knowledge: Are They Buying What We're Selling?" *Innovative Higher Education* 35 (5): 343–358.

DARREN S. FULLERTON is the vice president for student affairs at Missouri Southern State University, Joplin.

4

A well-crafted syllabus can serve as an initial point of engagement for the Millennial student.

The Syllabus: A Place to Engage Students' Egos

Mark Canada

For many, a syllabus is the academic equivalent of an appliance manual. Everyone expects one, but reading it is another matter. A few compulsive sorts may pore over every letter. Others may refer to it only when there is a problem. Many may never look at it at all. A syllabus can be much more, however. A well-crafted syllabus can be the beginning of a promise fulfilled and part of the difference between just another course and one that changes lives.

Am I making too much of this simple document? Consider first the attitude that many students bring to their college courses. The author of one study of high school students has argued that the U.S. educational system tends to produce "robo-students" caught in the "grade trap." These students often wind up merely "doing school," developing strategies and even cheating to get the grades they believe they need to succeed in the larger world (Pope 2001, 4, 153–154). Furthermore, some researchers have suggested that Millennial students bring to their classes a sense of entitlement that constitutes, in Twenge's famous phrase, a "Generation Me" (Twenge et al. 2008; Greenberger et al. 2008). While such claims are by no means definitive (Trzesniewski and Donnellan 2008), there can be little doubt that the period of "emerging adulthood" is a "*self-focused* time of life" (Arnett 2007, 26). Many Millennial students, then, might evaluate opportunities with a direct question: "What's in it for me?"

Now, consider the role a syllabus can play in framing this opportunity. If students are asking, "What's in it for me?" the syllabus can provide

New Directions for Teaching and Learning, no. 135, Fall 2013 © Wiley Periodicals, Inc.
Published online in Wiley Online Library (wileyonlinelibrary.com) • DOI: 10.1002/tl.20062

compelling, inviting answers: self-discovery, a sense of fulfillment, and, yes, a better chance of succeeding in life, whatever "success" means to any given student. Through solid production and effective presentation of the syllabus, professors can engage Millennial students in a stimulating intellectual journey.

Tone and Style

If we want to craft a syllabus that will appeal to Millennial students' egos in productive ways, then we need to employ a style of plain language and a tone of friendliness and humility.

Plain and Direct Language. A style of direct language is important. For instance, if many of today's students are focused on themselves, then one way to engage them in the syllabus may be as simple as using the pronoun *you* frequently. The constant use of "you" directly reminds students of their role in the course.

Furthermore, without plain language, Millennial students likely will experience the academic jargon of a course syllabus as verbose and meaningless—*theoretical*, *paradigm*, and *empiricism* are not part of their vernacular. We can and should teach students the necessary language of the discipline in the course, certainly; but first we need to engage them in the academic enterprise. A plain language style in the course syllabus will be more accessible and can help to ensure that the students will still be with us when it comes time to define the language of our discipline.

Friendliness. Research suggests that a friendly tone in a syllabus leaves students with more positive feelings toward the professor. In a study that called on them to read two syllabi—the first with a friendly tone and the second with a less friendly tone—students responded that the professor supposedly behind the first syllabus was warmer and more approachable than the professor supposedly behind the second syllabus (Harnish and Bridges 2011). In turn, students who find the professor approachable, we can assume, are more likely to seek assistance from this professor than they otherwise would be. Millennial students might be especially attracted to such a professor, who is more likely to be affirming than one who comes across as unfriendly in the syllabus. Giving a syllabus a friendlier tone can be as simple as adding a few personal or affirming phrases. For instance, instead of saying, "If you need to contact me," the "friendly" syllabus said, "I welcome you to contact me." Instead of referring to "skills you should obtain," this syllabus said, "skills I hope you will obtain" (Harnish and Bridges 2011, 323).

Humility. After years of study, professors naturally know far more about their subjects than their students know, but this gap in knowledge does not have to entail a gap in the relationship. In *What the Best College Teachers Do*, Bain (2004) notes that some outstanding professors come across as fellow intellectual sojourners in awe of the universe, not masters talking down to tenderfeet. One teacher even confessed his own difficulties with the material to his students. This humble approach helps to establish the relationship of professor and students as equals—on some level, anyway. Both are reasonably intelligent human beings with natural curiosities about the world. One has traveled quite a bit farther than the other, but both are on the same road and together can reach some of the same milestones. As long as the student appreciates what the professor has to offer—more knowledge and experience, if not necessarily more basic intelligence or human value—the resulting relationship can be positive. A humble syllabus says to students, "I'm with you. In fact, I used to be you."

Conceptual Unity

Of course, a syllabus is more than a warm or glitzy invitation to a course. For one thing, it should spell out the basics regarding assignments, deadlines, and grades. The syllabus also serves an important pedagogical role, framing the assignments and class work as part of "an organized and meaningful journey" (Slattery and Carlson 2005, 159). The inclusion of all these nuts and bolts, along with the unifying blueprint, need not render the syllabus lifeless. If the contents are carefully crafted to create conceptual unity, then a syllabus can engage students.

Syllabus Introduction. The introduction to the syllabus can promote the professor's confidence in students' abilities. Expressing confidence in students is a positive force in general (Bain 2004), and an introduction in the syllabus may be an appropriate place to express belief in each student's internal genius (Knowlton 2010). "Before we begin, let's get one thing straight," I say in the introductions to some of my syllabi. "I want to see every one of you succeed."

The introduction to a syllabus is also an ideal place to establish a "natural critical learning environment" (Bain 2004, 99), where students encounter large and meaningful questions that they will have the opportunity to explore throughout the course. Every discipline has such questions. For example, "What constitutes a good life?" and "What makes us love other people?" will come naturally in some philosophy and psychology syllabi. A syllabus in a math course might raise questions to help students see the content as more than a "plug and chug" series of formulas and equations, emphasizing instead its logic and rationality. Especially if they employ the word *you*—as in "Why do your parents make you so crazy?"—these questions can be especially useful in engaging Millennial students.

Finally, professors may want to use the introduction to establish a dramatic theme or inspiring metaphor for the course. By likening the course to an expedition or a project, professors not only add interest and make the material more accessible but also emphasize each student's role in his or her learning. Some professors, for example, characterize their students as "seekers" (Canada 2000, 35; Knowlton 2010, 78). Putting students in the driver's seat—or the captain's chair or the project manager's role, as the case may be—is sound pedagogy (Bain 2004). Here is the first paragraph of an introduction I use in a syllabus for a literature course:

> Imagine a road trip that could take you all over America, showing you exotic locales, introducing you to interesting characters, and dropping you in the middle of wild adventures. You will set sail on the high seas, stalk through the wilds of Virginia, and stroll down the streets of Philadelphia. You will meet powerful leaders and oppressed slaves, pious Christians and fiendish villains. You will experience passionate love and abject terror. Best of all, you will return home not exhausted and defeated, but refreshed and enlightened.

Road trips, relationships, jobs, and sports are all useful metaphors, which can help move students from the worlds they know and value to the academic realm we are introducing to them.

Course Objectives. A natural follow-up to the introduction in the syllabus is a list of objectives for the course. Teachers already appreciate "critical thinking," "historical forces," and "scientific principles"; however, objectives phrased in these terms are not likely to resonate with Millennial students, at least not if presented without any reference to what they perceive as the real world, namely jobs, money, relationships, and personal interests (Adams 2005).

The very notion that course objectives will center on learning is a key point, as it can help adjust the "consumer mentality" that leaves some students with the idea that courses are mere sources of credit hours or grades (O'Brien, Mills, and Cohen 2008). By simply helping students see how the learning in the course can help them with their own practical concerns, teachers can make a case for their courses. They might summarize studies showing that employers highly value communication skills or might articulate the value of "deep," "disciplinary," or "genuine" understanding (Bain 2004, 40; Gardner 1991, 9). Other possible approaches include encouraging students to set their own course goals (Lavoie 2007; Slattery and Carlson 2005).

Grading. Grades are the bane of any professor's existence. No one ever went into this profession to call balls and strikes, but umpires we are. While discussing grades in the syllabus is only fair, professors should take care to put them in perspective, explaining that grades are not ends in themselves, but merely an imperfect means for identifying successful learning. This approach might resonate with students who wish to be more learning-oriented (Pollio and Beck 2000). To minimize concern about grades, a professor might want to preface the description of the grading system with a statement like this one:

> When you go to the gym, do you ask others to rate your form or give you a score for how much you can lift? When you play the piano, do you ask your family to write a review of your performance? If you're like me and most other people, you do such things because you enjoy them and want to

improve, not because you are looking for a rating or a score. This course does involve grades; but when I assign those grades, I promise to do so conscientiously, applying the standards and criteria that are listed in this syllabus. Through this approach, the grade that you earn should provide an indication of my judgments about your learning.

Such a statement not only puts the emphasis on the learning and not the grades but also assures students that grades will be based on meaningful criteria—a useful message for students who suspect that knowledge is really a matter of opinion (Lippmann, Bulanda, and Wagenaar 2009). As the passage implies, professors can further combat this suspicion by making sure that the standards and criteria are stated clearly in the syllabus. Professors also should build assignments into the grading section of the syllabus that proclaim the importance of students applying the criteria and standards to their own work as a self-evaluation. Including this in the syllabus can help combat Adams's (2005) concern that students sometimes put more emphasis on effort than professors do. Promoting self-evaluation in the syllabus provides opportunities to think beyond effort alone.

Creating Early-Semester Engagement with the Syllabus

Even the best syllabus is worthless to the student who never reads it. While professors cannot force students to read anything, they can encourage them to engage with the syllabus, just as they would ask students to engage with a poem or an academic argument. Deep engagement will help students absorb the messages within the syllabus. For starters, professors can take a few minutes to walk students through the syllabus on the first day of class, taking care to complement its messages about big questions and promises with their oral remarks, expressions, gestures, and tone of voice.

Professors could ask students to begin weighing in on the big questions, first on paper and then out loud with others in the class. A brief writing assignment can extend the reflection outside the class, giving students an additional opportunity to reflect on the objectives and assignments described in the syllabus. For instance, biology professors might ask students to respond in writing to a question like this one: "How do you foresee using your knowledge of biology in your career, hobbies, or personal life?" In this way the assignment can call on students to move from the syllabus to some personal goals (Slattery and Carlson 2005). This type of assignment early in the semester can serve as a point for reflection and growth monitoring throughout the semester, thereby emphasizing the role of the syllabus as something other than a static document.

Conclusion

Business professionals know the power of the executive summary. Lawyers spend hours carefully crafting the opening statement. Conductors detail every nuance of the overture. It is time that professors take full advantage of their first written contact with students. Whatever its reputation, the syllabus need not be an opportunity wasted. A syllabus that is well crafted and meaningfully presented can shift the Millennial students' question from "What's in it for me?" to "What role should I play in discovering what's in it for me?"

References

Adams, J. B. 2005. "What Makes the Grade? Faculty and Student Perceptions." *Teaching of Psychology* 32 (1): 21–24.

Arnett, J. J. 2007. "Suffering, Selfish, Slackers? Myths and Reality about Emerging Adults." *Journal of Youth and Adolescence* 36: 23–29.

Bain, K. 2004. *What the Best College Teachers Do.* Cambridge, MA: Harvard University Press.

Canada, M. 2000. "Students as Seekers in Online Courses." In *Principles of Effective Teaching in the Online Classroom*, edited by R. E. Weiss, B. W. Speck, and D. S. Knowlton, 35–40. San Francisco: Jossey-Bass.

Gardner, H. 1991. *The Unschooled Mind: How Children Think and How Schools Should Teach.* New York: Basic Books.

Greenberger, E., J. Lessard, C. Chen, and S. P. Farruggia. 2008. "Self-Entitled College Students: Contributions of Personality, Parenting, and Motivational Factors." *Journal of Youth and Adolescence* 37 (10): 1192–1204.

Harnish, R. J., and K. R. Bridges. 2011. "Effect of Syllabus Tone: Students' Perceptions of Instructor and Course." *Social Psychology of Education* 14 (3): 319–330.

Knowlton, D. S. 2010. "Take Out the Tests, and Hide the Grades; Add the Spiritual with All Voices Raised! Professor Explications and Students' Opinions of an Unconventional Classroom Milieu." *Critical Questions in Education* 1 (2): 70–93.

Lavoie, R. 2007. *The Motivation Breakthrough: 6 Secrets to Turning on the Tuned-Out Child.* New York: Touchstone.

Lippmann, S., R. Bulanda, and T. Wagenaar. 2009. "Student Entitlement." *College Teaching* 57 (4): 197–204.

O'Brien, J. G., B. J. Mills, and M. W. Cohen. 2008. *The Course Syllabus: A Learning-Centered Approach.* San Francisco: Jossey-Bass.

Pollio, H. R., and H. P. Beck. 2000. "When the Tail Wags the Dog: Perceptions of Learning and Grade Orientation in, and by, Contemporary College Students and Faculty." *Journal of Higher Education* 71 (1): 84–102.

Pope, D. C. 2001. *Doing School: How We Are Creating a Generation of Stressed Out, Materialistic, and Miseducated Students.* New Haven, CT: Yale University Press.

Slattery, J. M., and J. F. Carlson. 2005. "Preparing an Effective Syllabus: Current Best Practices." *College Teaching* 53 (4): 159–164.

Trzesniewski, K. H., and M. B. Donnellan. 2008. "Is 'Generation Me' Really More Narcissistic Than Previous Generations?" *Journal of Personality* 76 (4): 903–918.

Twenge, J. M., S. Konrath, J. D. Foster, W. K. Campbell, and B. J. Bushman. 2008. "Egos Inflating over Time: A Cross-Temporal Metaanalysis of the Narcissistic Personality Inventory." *Journal of Personality* 76: 875–901.

MARK CANADA is professor of English and acting dean of the College of Arts and Sciences at the University of North Carolina at Pembroke.

5

This chapter offers strategies for engaging Millennial students in ways that affirm, rather than challenge, students' egos.

Facilitating Class Sessions for Ego-Piercing Engagement

Stephen Lippmann

Because of the characteristics and traits that set Millennials apart from their predecessors, traditional teaching techniques and pedagogies increasingly are ineffective tools in the college classroom. Exams, term papers, and other traditional assignments can leave students overly anxious about their grades and performance, while not paying particularly close attention to their learning. Lectures that simply present information in a unidirectional format not only are usually boring—indeed, students' attention appears to decline after about 15 minutes of lecture (Svinicki and McKeachie 2010)— but also are poor uses of classroom time for students who are accustomed to accessing basic information anytime, anywhere. Furthermore, lectures center attention completely on the professor, increasing the social and psychological distance between professors and students, among students, and even introspectively within a student. Professors who fail to engage Millennial students frequently and meaningfully in class run the risk of losing them to a variety of distractions on their smartphones or laptops.

Student engagement is applied widely to a variety of contexts, yet it is often poorly defined. The very characteristics of Millennials that make traditional approaches ineffective can allow for meaningful engagements in classroom dynamics and processes. True engagement during class will cause students to develop a deeper understanding of course material, use course content to challenge previously held beliefs and values (and vice versa), appreciate other students' perspectives, and think about how their own perspectives are situated in a universe of competing perspectives. In

NEW DIRECTIONS FOR TEACHING AND LEARNING, no. 135, Fall 2013 © Wiley Periodicals, Inc.
Published online in Wiley Online Library (wileyonlinelibrary.com) • DOI: 10.1002/tl.20063

this chapter, I suggest during-class strategies for engaging Millennial students on multiple levels.

Require and Grade Participation

Given the traits and characteristics of Millennial students, requiring participation can be an increasingly important and effective tool in helping students fuse themselves both with course content and with other learners. Requiring participation sends a strong signal to students that this type of fusion through participation is an important part of the class and a prerequisite for learning (Barr and Tagg 1995). With this perspective in mind, requiring participation can be the first step in letting students know that their voices matter toward the goal of making the classroom "work." No longer should they expect success by just showing up; instead, they need to remain engaged, think about the ways in which they understand the material, and contribute their own thoughts to the class in an effort to take ownership of that material.

In the social sciences and humanities, professors must give students the space that allows them to contribute their own experiences and ideas, instead of just repeating definitions or stock examples. Once that space is given, professors can require students to connect course concepts with their own lives—which are personally meaningful to Millennials. In math and science classrooms, it may be more difficult for students to contribute life experiences, but professors in those disciplines can establish the expectation of students sharing their own reasoning, through worked examples or scientific argumentation, for instance.

If expected and required, then participation should be graded. Initially, grading participation may seem counterproductive. After all, Millennials have grown up in an environment in which they are rewarded and praised for anything and everything, as the "trophy generation" moniker implies. There is evidence that Millennials are carrying these expectations with them as they leave the youth soccer field and enter the workforce (Alsop 2008). Some might argue that grading participation simply reinforces this pattern of rewarding students for something they should be doing anyway. I set this argument aside because grading participation can formally reinforce the message that participation is a significant and important part of the class. A variety of schemes exist for grading participation (see, for instance, Bean and Peterson 1998).

The requirement and grading of participation should neither be a surprise nor be antagonistic. Early in the semester, the professor should describe this component of the course and explain how it will be graded. Throughout the semester, professors must remind students why participation is important toward student learning. More important than simply posting participation grades, professors must give qualitative feedback to students. This way, students know where they stand and, more important, how they can improve their participation.

Learn and Use Students' Names

When professors address students by name, they are bridging a psychological divide that separates them from students. Instead of simply pointing, nodding, or mumbling a depersonalized "you" in the direction of an anonymous face, calling students by name sends a powerful signal of care (Nilson 2010). Using students' names demonstrates "personal investment in your students' well-being" (McKinney 2006), a characteristic that Millennials have come to expect in authority figures (Strauss and Howe 2007). Learning students' names should be an achievable goal for many, given the widespread availability of online photo rosters. For those who continue to have trouble, two useful guides have been provided by McKinney (2006) and Nilson (2010).

More than just calling on students by name, professors should weave students' names and ideas into the tapestry of the course. When lecturing, professors can reiterate previous student comments and examples: "Sally, does this point that I've just made about Chapter 5 bear any resemblance to the study abroad experience in France you told us about earlier?" As a result, students are more likely to feel that their comments continue to contribute to learning. When facilitating discussions, professors can help students think about the structure of the various contributions to the discussion: "How does Emma's story from her work experience connect to Paul's earlier comment that old organizations are more difficult to change?" As students are encouraged to consider their contributions in light of their classmates' contributions, their connections to both content and others are increased, thereby better engaging them at a meaningful level.

Invoke the Orienting Reflex

An orienting reflex is a response to ideas and information that is novel, surprising, complex, confusing, and disorienting (Berlyne 1961). When students encounter these types of ideas, which often conflict with their current knowledge or past experience, they tend to actively seek out new information or search for new patterns and relationships within existing information. The goal of this response is to restore their own sense of familiarity, certainty, and mastery.

The invocation of this orienting reflex is particularly applicable to teaching. Professors should examine their existing course content for material that can be presented in ways that introduce novelty, surprise, uncertainty, incongruity, conflict, and other manners that stimulate the orienting reflex (Kopp 2010). Beyond an examination of course content, matters of pedagogical style also can induce the orienting reflex in productive ways.

NEW DIRECTIONS FOR TEACHING AND LEARNING • DOI: 10.1002/tl

Inject Humor. The injection of humor in a sphere typically considered to be devoted to the serious, if not somber, pursuit of knowledge can invoke the orienting reflex by making students rethink their relationship to professors, the classroom, and learning (Torok, McMorris, and Lin 2004). I will, at times, overexaggerate my own unfamiliarity or confusion with popular culture, which provides opportunity for students to enjoy a chuckle at my expense. I have had great success in leveraging this type of humor not only to humanize myself, but also to allow students the opportunity to teach me about their values and their own sense of enjoyment in various elements of pop culture. Because I teach sociology, these discussions that begin in humor often advance course themes and objectives. All disciplines, though, have opportunities for professors to humanize themselves through humor, and Millennial students can reorient themselves to classrooms by seeing their professors in a new way.

Be Provocative. In a class on gender and stratification, I have had success making statements that temporarily shock (at least some) students and press them to argue with me and articulate an alternative explanation. When discussing the gender gap in pay or test scores, for example, I intentionally offer misdirection by suggesting that men very well may be better workers or smarter than women. I can typically count on at least a few students to actively challenge this facile explanation. Once they do, I subtly help them to articulate more nuanced explanations for social phenomena.

Approaches that lead to provocative moments within class sessions provide a unique way to force students to ask themselves both where they stand on an issue and whether they are willing to speak up and voice their standing. Provocative approaches can orient students not only with relation to content, but also in relation to their own constitutions and willingness to offer their worldviews in the face of injustice. This appreciation of their own identities and how they relate to "the other" is a major component of a healthy ego.

Correct Common Belief. Some students are unwilling to entertain new information that may contradict their worldviews or challenge their current understanding of course material. The conflict between common belief and known truth can provide opportunity for professors to invoke the orienting reflex as a way of helping students. One way to achieve this conflict in productive ways that allows students to reorient themselves is through a combination of anomalous data or cases and professor guidance (Sandoval 1995).

For example, in a course on social problems, students typically have opinions that likely are influenced by the mass media. Many students are conditioned to think that tragedies like child abductions and school shootings are increasingly ubiquitous risks facing children. In discussions of these issues, I typically spend some time allowing students to sound off with their opinions. The class quickly gets comfortable in their common belief that the moral fabric of the world is disintegrating around them. At this point, I will present unlabeled statistics about the risk of such an event occurring compared with the risk of some other, more common event (e.g., living in poverty and dying from a lightning strike). I ask students to label each frequency according to their beliefs. Students are usually wrong and assign higher frequencies to social problems that receive a lot of media coverage. After I reveal the true risks of these events, we have a discussion to make sense of why we fear the things that we do. Such discussions can also lead to consideration of how we know the things that we claim to know.

This approach can take advantage of guidance as offered by Ehrlich and Zoltek (2006). We go beyond simply telling students that their answers (and not the students personally) are wrong. We have allowed for discussion of why the answers were wrong. Students' incorrect opinions become a teaching opportunity to activate the orienting reflex.

Conclusion

As professors from previous generations struggle to understand and make sense of Millennials, those professors might describe students in terms and tones that range from the incredulous to the downright distrustful and antagonistic (Twenge 2006). For those professors, the strategies offered in this chapter may seem naive and a dodge of the actual problem. I suggest, though, that these negative views of Millennials are too narrow. Data demonstrate that Millennials are more optimistic than older adults and are more engaged in their communities and in politics than many from older generations. They are also described as more ambitious, collaborative, and confident in their abilities to solve the world's problems (Winograd and Hais 2011). Many of these traits provide the raw materials that are needed if professors are to build upon opportunities for helping each student to develop a strong identity through meaningful engagement.

References

Alsop, R. 2008. *The Trophy Kids Grow Up: How the Millennial Generation Is Shaking Up the Workplace.* San Francisco: Jossey-Bass.

Barr, R. B., and J. Tagg. 1995. "From Teaching to Learning: A New Paradigm for Undergraduate Education." *Change* 27 (November/December): 12–25.

Bean, J. C., and D. Peterson. 1998. "Grading Classroom Participation." In *Changing the Way We Grade Student Performance: Classroom Assessment and the New Learning Paradigm*, New Directions for Teaching and Learning, no. 74., edited by R. S. Anderson and B. W. Speck, 33–40. San Francisco: Jossey-Bass.

Berlyne, D. E. 1961. "Conflict and the Orienting Reaction." *Journal of Experimental Psychology* 65 (5): 476–483.

Erlich, R., and S. Zoltek. 2006. "It's Wrong Not to Tell Students When They're Wrong." *Journal of College Science Teaching* 35 (4): 8–10.

Kopp, T. W. 2010. "What Is Intellectual Curiosity?" Presented at the Lily Conference on College Teaching, Oxford, OH, November.

McKinney, M. 2006. "What's Your Name Again?" *Insidehighered.com*, February. Accessed September 20, 2011. http://www.insidehighered.com/workplace/2006/02/13 /mckinney.

Nilson, L. B. 2010. *Teaching at Its Best: A Research-Based Resource for College Instructors*, 3rd ed. San Francisco: Jossey-Bass.

Sandoval, J. 1995. "Teaching in Subject Matter Areas: Science." *Annual Review of Psychology* 46 (February): 355–374.

Strauss, N., and W. Howe. 2007. *Millennials Go to College*, 2nd ed. Great Falls, VA: LifeCourse Associates.

Svinicki, M., and W. J. McKeachie. 2010. *McKeachie's Teaching Tips: Strategies, Research, and Theory for College and University Teachers*, 13th ed. Boston: Houghton Mifflin.

Torok, S. E., R. F. McMorris, and W. Lin. 2004. "Is Humor an Appreciated Teaching Tool?" *College Teaching* 52 (1): 14–20.

Twenge, J. M. 2006. *Generation Me*. New York: Free Press.

Winograd, M., and D. C. Hais. 2011. *Millennial Momentum: How a New Generation Is Reshaping America*. New Brunswick, NJ: Rutgers University Press.

STEPHEN LIPPMANN *is associate professor of sociology at Miami University in Oxford, Ohio.*

6

This chapter describes an assignment that immerses Millennial students in discipline-based politics and policy as a means of helping them meaningfully connect with content.

Immersion in Political Action: Creating Disciplinary Thinking and Student Commitment

Karen Kelly

Introduction

Students often enter their undergraduate studies without really understanding the discipline they seek to join. In my discipline of nursing, for instance, many students are shocked to discover the sciences they must study as prerequisites to their nursing course work. Others enter the nursing program with a "soap opera" image of professional practices, far removed from the complex realities of the health care system and nursing profession.

In disciplines where students enter their college programs with naive and simplistic views, professors can help by immersing students in activities that require disciplinary thinking—the way that professionals in the discipline think, not just the content that they know. In my case, I use an assignment that provides opportunities for students to become engaged in a variety of political activities that are designed to shape their understanding of health policy. This chapter provides an overview of this assignment and its implementation. My experiences suggest that assignments like this one can promote disciplinary thinking in Millennial students. At the end of the chapter, I offer advice for faculty members across disciplines.

NEW DIRECTIONS FOR TEACHING AND LEARNING, no. 135, Fall 2013 © Wiley Periodicals, Inc.
Published online in Wiley Online Library (wileyonlinelibrary.com) • DOI: 10.1002/tl.20064

Millennial Students, Immersive Activities, and Nursing

In cases where the content of a new Millennial student's discipline is as necessary as it is alien, immersion activities that promote disciplinary thinking are ideal. When it comes to processing large volumes of information, Millennial students have a propensity for multitasking and an aversion to single activities that are isolated from a larger context (Pardue and Morgan 2008). Millennials benefit from instruction that comes in interactive formats (Twenge 2009). Engaging Millennial students in fieldwork, then, might beneficially match Millennials' needs with productive entry points into the discipline. Siegal and Kagan (2012) found this to be true in gerontology studies, for instance.

Health policy and the political processes that shape it are alien content for most Millennial students, as these topics reach far outside of their personal experiences. For many Millennials, political action is not a common experience, and *health policy* is just a phrase they have heard; they have little context by which to give meaning to the role health policy plays in their lives. Yet, health policy and politics are sorely needed knowledge bases within a nursing program. Future nurses need to learn about the basic elements of the American health care system, how it operates or fails to operate effectively in meeting the needs of the population, and even how to shape the health care system as citizen lobbyists.

An interdisciplinary component is important within nursing. It is a useful irony that interdisciplinary thinking serves as a solid foundation of disciplinary thinking. Nursing education programs generally do well in preparing students for clinical practice, but they "are not generally effective in teaching ... social sciences, technology, and humanities" (Benner et al. 2010, 12). The political activities assignment immerses students in a matrix of sociology, political science, history, and psychology, with an emphasis on both oral and verbal communication skills.

The Political Activities Assignment

The inspiration for the political activities assignment dates back to the 1984 presidential campaign, when a colleague and I taught an elective course for undergraduate students completing their baccalaureate degree in nursing (Schutzenhofer and Cannon 1986). Students were challenged to immerse themselves in the campaigns of the candidates of their choice, to write letters about health care issues, and to interview legislators and candidates. Over the years the assignment has evolved to the version that I now use.

Assignment Initiation. Prior to giving students the health policy assignment, I ask them to complete a self-assessment of their political savvy using a tool adapted from Goldwater and Zusy (1990). Among other things, this assessment determines students' knowledge of their elected representatives in the state legislature and Congress and their awareness of current legislative health care issues. The purpose of asking them to complete the survey is to establish a baseline of their current knowledge.

After all students have completed the assessment, I distribute a menu of suggested political activities. The items on the menu provide students with an opportunity to learn both what health policy is and how political processes shape the policies that influence the U.S. health care system. I invite students to suggest additional activities as opportunities that may not be on my menu list. Some examples of activities that I have used in the menu are:

- Interviewing legislators about health policy legislation
- Observing a session of the state legislature, a county board meeting, a county board of health meeting, or a city council/alderman meeting
- Writing letters to the editors of newspapers and newsmagazines on current health policy issues
- Attending selected community meetings or professional organization meetings where health policy issues are part of the agenda
- Working in political campaigns
- Attending meetings of the state board of nursing and state regulatory boards that deal with health policy issues

All of the menu items are meant to empower students to consider their own roles in political participation and in shaping health policy. A menu approach allows Millennials to select political activities that are meaningful to them, which heightens the likelihood that they will immerse themselves in these interactive opportunities.

Process-Based Planning. Students must provide evidence of envisioning and planning their completion of the menu items. For instance, students who plan to interview a legislator must provide me with a draft of their interview agenda and potential interview questions. Students who write a letter to a legislator or editor on health policy legislation must provide an outline or early draft of the letter.

This preparation does not occur in a vacuum. Part of preparation requires students to synthesize their plan with a variety of course materials, such as readings from textbooks, journal articles, trade publications, and so forth. I offer in-class lectures and create online podcasts on topics that might be relevant to the completion of their menu activities. For instance, the content within some of these lectures and podcasts explicitly addresses the complexities of the U.S. health care system.

The requirement of planning and connecting that plan to course content serves several purposes. Most prominently, it ensures that their plan is well conceived. For example, interviews on Medicare, a federal matter, have been proposed with state legislators; and letters on nurse licensure laws, a state matter, have been proposed to members of Congress. Planning provides an opportunity for timely correction of such problems.

Written Documentation and Reflection. In all cases, the completion of the menu item must result in a written document that serves as a report. In cases where completing the menu item inherently requires writing (e.g., a letter to the editor of a newspaper), that writing can serve as the report. In cases where the menu item is not an act of writing (e.g., attending a board meeting), students must write a report that includes a summary that details the chronology of events during the activity and a reflection about what the student learned from the activity. This reflection is the most important element of the report and serves as a self-assessment of learning. Reflection on the experience requires students to note their personal learning outcomes.

Assignment Outcomes. Engaging Millennials in a series of political activities brings politics and health policy to life for students. Through immersion into activities that they control, students learn the importance of speaking up about legislative and policy matters and the best processes for making one's voice heard. They learn how to be citizen lobbyists, advocating for themselves, their professions or disciplines, their families, and their communities. At the conclusion of the course, students again complete the self-assessment of their political savvy. Most students consistently report a gain of 10 to 15 points (out of 40 total) in political savvy.

The value of this assignment can be seen beyond test scores. While some students express an initial degree of trepidation about the assignment, they come to see the value in these political activities as a meaningful learning experience. One student wrote in an e-mail at the end of the semester: "I was terrified to write to my state representative, then excited to get a letter from him acknowledging my position on the issue." Another student, who had attended a county board of health meeting, wrote, "One of the board members was a neighbor of my parents. I realized that everyday people were serving on this important board. I was greeted by our neighbor and introduced to other board members."

Students express great pride in their personal growth as policy shapers: "Now I can talk about health care reform—and I know what I'm talking about." Another student expressed pride in her new role as an informed health care consumer who has authoritative resources to consult when she needs to make a decision in the future, including helping her grandmother with health care decisions.

Implications of Immersion Assignments

Students in a variety of disciplines might benefit from this kind of discipline-based immersion experience. To faculty members across disciplines, I offer the following advice:

- Traditional components are legitimate in an immersion assignment. Immersion assignments can be supported by lectures or teacher-provided resources. For instance, I provide students with guidance on how to write letters. Immersive assignments and academic tradition can work hand in hand.

- Draft submissions are important. Particularly because Millennials prefer multitasking, which can distract them from a linear focus toward assignment completion, requiring students to submit outlines, drafts, and other in-process artifacts can be useful. These submissions keep students focused and provide opportunity for just-in-time feedback that can help students improve their work.

- Immerse students where they are least comfortable. After all, if an immersive experience simply provides new sites for Millennial students to continue with routine and status quo learning, then that experience probably is not novel enough to support learning. The public sphere of politics, cultural tensions, and social justice disparity can be particularly useful realms of discipline-based immersion because those realms take students out of their comfort zones.

- Immersion not only can create depth within the experience, but also can expose students to breadth across disciplines. The immersion assignment that I designed combines the fields of nursing, political science, interpersonal communication, and sociology, just to name a few. Interdisciplinary experiences provide more opportunities for Millennial students to find meaning in the relationship of course material to their sense of self.

With this guidance, I believe that immersive, discipline-based activities can provide opportunities for Millennial students to discover that they can fuse their own thinking with the characteristic thinking that is distinctive of the discipline. In so doing, those students are likely to find more ego-grounded connections between their personal and professional identities.

References

Benner, P., M. Sutphen, V. Leonard, and L. Day. 2010. *Educating Nurses: A Call for Radical Transformation*. San Francisco: Jossey-Bass.

Goldwater, M., and M. J. L. Zusy. 1990. *Prescription for Nurses: Effective Political Action*. St. Louis, MO: Mosby.

Pardue, K. T., and P. Morgan. 2008. "Millennials Reconsidered: A New Generation, New Approaches, and Implications for Nursing Education." *Nursing Education Perspectives* 29 (2): 14–19.

Schutzenhofer, K. K., and S. B. Cannon. 1986. "Moving Nurses into the Political Process." *Nurse Educator* 11 (2): 26–28.

Siegal, B., and S. H. Kagan. 2012. "Teaching Psychological and Social Gerontology to Millennial Undergraduates." *Educational Gerontology* 38 (1): 20–29.

Twenge, J. M. 2009. "Generational Changes and Their Impact in the Classroom." *Medical Education* 43 (5): 398–405.

KAREN KELLY *is associate professor of nursing at Southern Illinois University Edwardsville. She also is director of the Continuing Education Department of Primary Care and Health Systems Nursing.*

7

This chapter describes the process and outcomes that follow from inviting students to explore deeper aspects of themselves through digital storytelling.

Selves, Lives, and Videotape: Leveraging Self-Revelation through Narrative Pedagogy

Alison G. Reeves

The Millennial generation varies culturally from previous generations of students and is most successful in classrooms that provide opportunities for "deep" thinking and learner-centered engagement (McGlynn 2007, 115). Professors can create such a classroom by capitalizing on "funds of knowledge," students' rich but hidden background stemming from their life in families, communities, and society (Moll et al. 1992, 133). One way to capitalize on these funds is to engage students in narrative pedagogy— the telling of their own life stories through personal histories, reflective narratives, and autobiographies. Narrative pedagogy promotes the "natural tendency to create stories to give coherence to the whole of the lived experience" (Garcia and Rossiter 2010, 1093) in ways that are epistemologically different from empirical or rational ways of knowing (Bruner 1991). Grounded in a focus on constructing knowledge of self, the social world, and culture, narrative pedagogy is authentically learner-centered and, therefore, highly engaging.

One increasingly popular form of narrative pedagogy is digital storytelling. A digital story is a "short, first person video-narrative created by combining recorded voice, still and moving images, and music or other sounds" (Center for Digital Storytelling 2011). Digital storytelling creates a compelling combination of the timeless allure of storytelling and current digital media. Digital storytelling "recognizes, honors, and encourages the

NEW DIRECTIONS FOR TEACHING AND LEARNING, no. 135, Fall 2013 © Wiley Periodicals, Inc.
Published online in Wiley Online Library (wileyonlinelibrary.com) • DOI: 10.1002/tl.20065

narrative meaning-making process as central to learning" (Rossiter and Garcia 2010, 38).

Digital Stories to Build a Collective Understanding of Culture

I have used a digital storytelling assignment in a foundations of education course for preservice teachers. My use of a digital storytelling assignment merges my goal of promoting in-depth understanding of course content with my love of creative expression in the classroom. At first, a digital story assignment was ambitious for me; as a "digital immigrant" rather than a "digital native" (Prensky, cited in McGlynn 2007, 57), I was unfamiliar with most of the technology required. My use of the assignment, though, provided opportunities for meaningful student learning by Millennial students.

Assignment Overview. The assignment is deceptively simple at first glance, as it invites students to demonstrate and share their understanding of the concept of culture by writing a personal narrative and presenting it in the form of a digital story: "Create a digital story that tells about your culture and its influence on you" with "at least 10 different images and an audio narration that complements the images." Students are given access to a computer lab, production software, equipment, and a tutorial that focuses on software usage. Many students are surprisingly anxious about their own technical skills. By providing training in the use of the software, I can help students set aside their own technical savvy as an issue and focus on the ideas that underlie the assignment.

I introduce this assignment by showing a few examples of digital stories, including my own digital story that explores the ways my rural, Protestant, working-class background shapes my values and beliefs and how the experience of being a first-generation college student fuels my passion for education reform. Admittedly, it is difficult to share my story, because I am revealing things about my life that students would likely never know otherwise. But sharing my story starts building the trust necessary for students to share stories with me and with their peers while demonstrating the expectation that they make a personal connection with the concept of culture and its powerful influence in each of our lives.

Office Meetings and Consultations. As students draft the text for their digital stories, many make appointments with me to talk about the assignment and their narratives. During our meetings, students express anxiety and overt resistance about an open-ended assignment that clearly requires synthesis of content, reflection on personal experience, and divergent thinking. Students are palpably uncomfortable being asked to construct knowledge, insecure about the value of the experiences and reflections they bring to the assignment, and unsure how to access their own creative powers.

While I can easily provide more resources, discuss concepts, and provide help with technology, helping students build agency toward constructing their personal understanding of their culture proves more difficult. At one meeting a student asked, "Where do you start unweaving a web you know?" Yet, even more difficult is helping students realize this assignment is, at its heart, entirely about them and that it cannot be completed without extended reflection on their lived experience, which differs noticeably from more familiar modes of self-representation such as using social media. During another meeting, a student expressed that she was "reluctant to share my home life because it is so blatantly immigrant and foreign. ... I am embarrassed and afraid." Such confessions provide me with the opportunity to admit that I feel that way too when I share my story. These moments of honesty allow me to explore with students the possibilities that reluctance and embarrassment provide in their future work as teachers. I've learned to trust that student resistance is an indication that deep learning is taking place.

During these meetings, I am often uncomfortable, too; while students inhabit the murky place of struggling to construct meaning through their narratives, I give up my authority over the concepts we are exploring. I cannot tell them what only they know. I do not have answers, only questions. Moving through our shared discomfort requires different approaches for various students, but it always starts with empathetic listening to understand where they are stuck and asking questions to help them move forward in their thinking and writing.

Commenting on Drafts. As students tentatively submit their first drafts of the text for their digital story, they make comments: "I'm not sure what you are looking for, and I'm not sure I understand what my culture is, but this is my best effort." "I don't have a culture. I'm just a typical American." "I've shared a really personal story. Let me know if it is too personal." "Can you write me as soon as you have read this? I really want some feedback." "I've asked you a ton of questions about my story; I hope there aren't too many."

It takes considerable time to read and comment on the narratives, but I am being trusted with a very important part of my students' lives, and my comments must reflect and extend that trust. I give feedback on the structure of the story, point out areas I feel are particularly engaging, and ask probing questions about things that seem to need elaboration. Because these narratives are designed to get students to explore the concept of culture, I comment on that specifically.

Students know in advance that they are the judge of when their story is finished and that I will read and comment on as many drafts as they want; the average student turns in his or her story to me three to six times before deciding it is finished. One student noted, "Once I got into it, I found it very difficult to stop but I had to stop to finish my movie."

The ongoing dialogue occurring while I am reading drafts of stories has immediate effects on my teaching, as well. As I read student narratives, I take notes about student understanding and use the notes to map students' collective awareness about sociocultural issues being discussed in class, creating an immediate window into student understanding with which to revise teaching emphases iteratively. I might note that several students are confused about the differences between the concepts of race, ethnicity, and nationality, or see evidence that many are struggling with health issues and realize that health status is an important form of diversity that we need to discuss more fully; I therefore change my plans for what we will read or discuss in class the next day. I see evidence of better understanding in subsequent drafts; the meaning-making process is reciprocal and dynamic.

Beyond content considerations, reading student stories allows me to know students more personally; the boundaries typically in place between professor and student become blurred. I shared a very personal story—now they are sharing very personal stories with me, and our relationship becomes richer. Student conversations with me reflect their new awareness of my life story: "I hope you'll understand that I need to turn this in late. I know you had to work in college, too"; "I wasn't sure I would graduate because no one in my family has; but if you could do it, I can do it." I've come to appreciate each student's life experience more fully. For example, when I learned that a student I had assumed was frequently late because of frivolous partying was in reality caring for his grandmother with Alzheimer's every moment he was not in class so his parents could work to pay for his education, my anger at his perceived incivility transformed into profound empathy. Knowing from his digital story that one young man had already lost one brother in Iraq intensified the way I felt when I learned that his only other brother was killed in a car accident; I reached out to him, even though it had been three years since I'd had him in class. The experience of sharing stories is both moving and humbling, inspiring new hopes and ideas while stripping away old assumptions.

Production.   As I observe students working in the computer lab to produce their stories, I frequently see them in a collective state of what Csikszentmihalyi (1990) would call "flow." Individually and in groups, students make revisions to their narratives; record and rerecord their stories to adjust the volume, pacing, and tone; thoughtfully examine family pictures, selecting and arranging them for continuity and cohesion; and ask each other for advice about music to include. During peak production weeks, some students commonly work in the lab for six to eight hours at a time. Other students request additional lab hours on weekends or during the evening.

Screening.   The digital stories are screened over several class meetings. The experience of watching is deeply personal and emotional; as we watch, we relate to the storyteller, each other, and ourselves. After each story is screened, students pause to take notes that they will use for a reflective writing exercise later. Some students get out of their seats to interact with the storyteller before we move on to the next story. I have witnessed high fives for the young woman who overcame multiple disabilities to make it to college and now wants to be a teacher to help kids like her succeed. There have been tears for classmates whose views have been indelibly shaped by serving in recent wars. Other viewers get lost in deep reflection. Are they thinking "that is me" when a student tells a story of growing up in abject poverty and shows pictures of the tiny, dilapidated house in which he grew up? Do some students feel spiritually moved when a student talks about the deep influence of her own religion?

Students' written reflections demonstrate that they come away with a much richer understanding of cultural diversity; and, importantly, that understanding is personally felt: "There are deep stories in everyone's lives." "I learned just how culturally different we all are even though we are in the 'same' place, and that is shocking to me." "You think you know things. Then after you watch the stories you realize there is so much more to learn."

Narrative Pedagogy across the Higher Education Curriculum

Narrative pedagogy is an obvious fit for engaging students in the humanities and social sciences. Personal narrative is a well-explored tactic in teaching the foundations of education (Ingram 2009). But there is growing acknowledgement of its pedagogical potential in other disciplines. In the field of nursing, for instance, narrative pedagogy is a fresh pedagogical approach that allows "teachers and students to publicly share and interpret stories of their learned experiences," such as "caring for another person or being cared for" (Ironside 2003, 123). In an accounting program, a storytelling project used instructor- and student-developed nonaccounting stories to foster critical thinking, student engagement, and ultimately deep understanding of accounting concepts (Miley 2009).

The following suggestions offer a starting place for considering how narrative pedagogy might fit in various disciplines:

- Start with research. The growing literature about the ways narrative pedagogy is used in higher education both in face-to-face classrooms and in virtual settings can help you determine how narrative pedagogy might inspire student engagement in your discipline.
- Select a prompt that is appropriately complex and allows for divergent thinking. Narrative pedagogy is at its heart a means for helping students construct meaning and works best with complex concepts that are worthy of extended engagement. The use of prompts that culminate in right answers will not be useful.
- Focus on process, not product. Much of the learning that takes place is not visible in the final product of a personal narrative. Even when the final product may not be as strong as hoped for, you should consider the valuable learning that occurred throughout the process.

- Require students to synthesize their lives with content. Narrative pedagogy is not a simplistic forum for students to learn only about themselves at the expense of learning about content. A well-designed personal narrative assignment should require students to fuse themselves and their lived experiences with that which is beyond the self.
- Rethink your role in the classroom. Narrative pedagogy fosters knowledge construction that is grounded in a student's ability to make a personal connection with content and to arrive at unique understandings. This may challenge both your epistemological beliefs and your definition of teaching.

Conclusion

Narrative pedagogy challenges us to consider the integral role of narrative in human learning and acknowledges the critical contributions of place and perspective in the meaning-making process. Narrative pedagogy has the potential to deeply engage Millennial students at a personal level while promoting critical thinking about course content. Digital storytelling as a narrative pedagogy can leverage students' ego needs in ways that defamiliarize the self, and soon turns mere solipsism inside out.

References

Bruner, J. 1991. "The Narrative Construction of Reality." *Critical Inquiry* 18: 1–19.
Center for Digital Storytelling. 2011. *Organizational website*. Accessed August 2, 2011. http://www.storycenter.org/index1.html.
Csikszentmihalyi, M. 1990. *Flow: The Psychology of Optimal Experience*. New York: Harper & Row.
Garcia, P., and M. Rossiter. 2010. "Digital Storytelling as Narrative Pedagogy." In *Proceedings of Society for Information Technology & Teacher Education International Conference*, edited by D. Gibson and B. Dodge, 1091–1097. Chesapeake, VA: AACE.
Ingram, I. 2009. "Creative Maladjustment: Engaging Personal Narrative to Teach Diversity and Social Justice." *Journal of Women in Educational Leadership* 7 (1): 7–22.
Ironside, P. 2003. "Trying Something New: Implementing and Evaluating Narrative Pedagogy." *Nursing Education Perspectives* 24 (3): 122–128.
McGlynn, A. P. 2007. *Teaching Today's College Students: Widening the Circle of Success*. Madison, WI: Atwood Publishing.
Miley, F. 2009. "The Storytelling Project: Innovating to Engage Students in Their Learning." *Higher Education Research and Development* 28 (4): 357–369.
Moll, L., C. Amanti, D. Neff, and N. Gonzalez. 1992. "Funds of Knowledge for Teaching: Using a Qualitative Approach to Connect Homes and Classrooms." *Theory into Practice* 31 (2): 132–140.
Rossiter, M., and P. Garcia. 2010. "Digital Storytelling: A New Player on the Narrative Field." In *Narrative Perspectives on Adult Education*, New Directions for Adult and Continuing Education, no. 126, edited by M. Rossiter and M. C. Clark, 37–48. San Francisco: Jossey-Bass.

ALISON G. REEVES is assistant professor of educational administration at Southern Illinois University Edwardsville.

8

This chapter provides strategies for harnessing the power of social media to better help Millennial students connect with course content.

Activating Ego Engagement through Social Media Integration in the Large Lecture Hall

C. Michael Elavsky

Consider: A large lecture hall on a big university campus. Hundreds of students waiting passively for another lecture to commence. Three times a week, each lecture's routine is similar to the previous one: Esteemed person enters the room, notebooks open, lights dim, overhead projection fires up, and microphone crackles in its initial delivery; the lecture commences. All heads bow, copying diligently every note and utterance. Only rarely are questions raised by random students who usually cannot be heard throughout the room. Now and again, disturbances—chattering, a laugh, a student packing up to leave—interrupt the delivery, evoking at times reproachful remarks about said interlocutors and disrupters. Students mechanically formulate their notes, the information to be memorized and regurgitated on a future exam.

Students—whose ID numbers are often more important than their names—perform abstract and hollow tasks that supersede the making of meaningful connections between the course material and their evolving life perspective. Rarely is there an inclination to question this routine, much less consider the larger purposes of the processes in which students are enmeshed. The professor continually reads from the transparency overheads while students dutifully copy down each word. This was my experience as a student in 1985.

Fast-forward to today and the scene is much the same—except now, students' attention is attuned to their ubiquitous laptops, tablets, and smartphones. Professors often see these devices as adversaries that disrupt

New Directions for Teaching and Learning, no. 135, Fall 2013 © Wiley Periodicals, Inc.
Published online in Wiley Online Library (wileyonlinelibrary.com) • DOI: 10.1002/tl.20066

classroom norms and promote addle-minded entertainment and apathy. Many professors respond to these devices by asking students to turn them off and set them aside, leaving students only to bow in reverence continually to get through the course by writing down those utterances of the esteemed in longhand—just as it was done in 1985, though the professor now reads from PowerPoint instead of acetate transparencies.

It does not have to be this way, and I argue that it is the very presence of Millennial students' "disruptive" technologies that offers the potential and promise for breaking through disengagement and unproductive routine. This is particularly true to the extent that professors can harness a social component to mobile devices and capitalize on the power of social media.

Ubiquitous Technologies in Perspective

For many, the omnipresence of mobile devices and social media platforms in Millennial students' lives represents the general decline in student attention spans and learning capacities. But while Facebook, text, Internet games, and other technologies certainly provide avenues for Millennial students to more effectively tune out during class, they simultaneously offer avenues for students to more effectively tune in, if only the technologies are employed with foresight and care (Elavsky 2012).

Policing the room against mobile technology incursion is to me, in a word, pointless; doing so is an updated version of stopping the passing of notes in class. We live in a world of ubiquitous media, and professors must critically rethink how those media will relate both to their own teaching and to Millennial students' learning. Simply embracing the power of these new technologies and platforms is certainly no shortcut for instructional quality. However, the interactive capacities of many mobile devices possess a potential to dramatically reconfigure the social dynamics of the classroom, providing a more meaningful experience for students and professors alike. The reconfiguration begins with a willingness to explore an interactive classroom driven by social media. Such a classroom not only can enable student voices and reinvigorate human relationships but also can broaden the ways that knowledge and the parameters of one's education are ultimately produced.

Ubiquitous Media in the College Classroom

In this section, I describe three different approaches that I have used for integrating contemporary technologies into large courses. The first and second approaches deal with the use of media inside the lecture hall. The third deals with the use of media outside of class. Each meets some of the unique needs of Millennial students.

Media-Driven Lectures. During class, the integration of students' mobile tools can help restructure lectures to foster an atmosphere that is more intimate, inviting, and engaging. Certainly, I use presentation software, such as PowerPoint or Prezi (www.prezi.com); but I shape the content of these presentations to ask questions or solicit reactions to controversial ideas.

Furthermore, I encourage students to utilize the Internet access on their mobile devices to check and challenge my talking points, explore related ideas, and connect course content to current events. In my experience, encouraging students to fact-check controversial premises and consider alternative views actually induces them to engage more concretely and invest themselves in the learning process. This use of media as a research tool turns the dialogue internal and allows them to, in essence, check themselves.

A more social dimension of this approach exists, too. My teaching assistants and I circulate around the room with microphones, encouraging student sharing about what they learn as they check both the facts and the points in the lecture and go beyond my presentation to develop more broadly synthesized ideas. This use of during-class dialogue fundamentally offsets the unidirectional tendencies of the large lecture classroom. Their mobile tools become support that motivates open conversation and elevates students' voices in a classroom space where they normally are muted. The elevation of student voice can enhance Millennial students' commitment to various types of content (Knowlton 2010).

Twitter in the Classroom. While questions and comments flow from the microphones swimming across the sea of students in the room, a during-class multiplatform discussion can be created to allow questions and observations to simultaneously simmer overhead, adding intellectual color to the classroom commentary in ways that ultimately extend the range of thinking, reflection, and participation.

Inspired by a story in *Time* magazine about the use of Twitter in megachurches to facilitate communication between the pulpit and congregation (Rochman 2009), I introduced Twitter in my large lecture class as a channel for students to voice their comments and ask questions in real time. By asking students to include a designated hashtag (e.g., "#PSU110") in their tweets, it is easy to aggregate all tweeted contributions and project them overhead. This approach opens even more space for greater student participation. After all, only one student can have the literal microphone at any given moment, but Twitter gives all students a simultaneous microphone. I found that this use of Twitter complemented and augmented class sessions (see, for instance, Elavsky, Mislan, and Elavsky 2011). Certainly, other tools, such as Harvard Moderator (http://cyber.law.harvard.edu/questions /chooser.php), can serve this same purpose; but as Millennial students are familiar with Twitter, I have found Twitter to be more convenient.

Students use a variety of strategies to contribute to the Twitter stream. Some post reactions to what was said in class or share a URL to support or rebut a point made in the more official discussion that I am facilitating.

NEW DIRECTIONS FOR TEACHING AND LEARNING • DOI: 10.1002/tl

Other students expand the ideas being discussed in class by tweeting examples and questions. Still others share personal experiences and anecdotes that deeply and meaningfully—all within 140 characters, mind you—personalize the connections between themselves and the topics under discussion. The anonymity of Twitter uniquely affords some students with particular opportunities to contribute sensitive perspectives. For instance, Iraq war veterans have shared their controversial views about warfare without being publicly identified in class. These approaches create salient additions to the discussion; watching the evolution of these multimodal conversations has been a marvel to behold.

The Twitter stream becomes a complementary backdrop to, not a distraction from, the engagement stimulated in class. Still, the multiple dimensions of these interactions—professor lecture, students' comments into microphones, and the Twitter stream—can lead to a somewhat chaotic discussion. Therefore, I suggest that professors devote the last five minutes of class to summing up key points that have emerged while encouraging the students to continue the discussion beyond the classroom.

Social Media Outside of Class. Certainly, professors commonly integrate discussion boards as a social medium into their classroom, and many sources can provide insight on their use (see, for instance, Knowlton 2004; Matheson, Wilkinson, and Gilhooly 2012; Rollag 2010). But Facebook, Spaaze, Harvard Moderator, Google Apps, and other social media platforms can be equally well integrated into college courses (Elavsky 2012). For instance, my students have used the virtual bulletin board Spaaze (www.spaaze.com) to collaboratively produce cyber-study guides. This use of social media provides an opportunity for Millennial students simultaneously to aim for their own enlightened self-interests of higher grades, while more communally contributing to the aggregate knowledge of their peers.

Also, in my class, students can submit potential exam questions for which they receive extra credit if their questions are used. Previously, these questions were submitted individually without a lot of critical reflection on their efficacy or design. Encouraging them to work together as a class on this exercise using Google applications, such as Google Documents and Google+, has produced a definitive increase in the quality of the proposed questions. Students are no longer just writing questions; they are using the media to discuss the questions, and they are including me in the conversations. Through these platforms, they have the opportunity to debate, discuss, and ultimately contribute to the design of the exam, while simultaneously reflecting more broadly on what they are really learning in the class.

Facebook is another valuable social medium that I urge professors to consider using in their courses. There is a Facebook page for my large lecture hall course. The members of that page total over 500 and include both current and former students. Because Facebook is widely used by Millennial students, integrating it into communication protocols of my class sends a subtle message that there is virtue in synthesizing their social space with purposeful learning space.

Crucial to all of the preceding is professor participation, not as an authority figure or nemesis but as a colleague and, dare I say, "friend." To this end, I am active in these virtual platforms, regularly posting in ways that move beyond didactic commentary. I regularly will reply to students' Facebook posts, insert points for consideration into their Google docs, or contribute tweets to a conversation that has continued after class. I am careful to ensure that my comments do not dominate the discourse but, instead, cultivate new and more meaningful forms of connection between professor and student. Through my contributions, I intend to promote the tenets that we are in this together, that we have much to learn from each other, that learning can take many shapes, and that social media can assist us in collectively learning, if we honestly invest.

A Note to the Detractors

Integrating new technologies into pedagogy has detractors. In this section, I address three common counterarguments to the implementation of the strategies that I have suggested.

Social Media Provides a Forum for Inappropriate Expressions. Some argue that the formal use of social media in the classroom elevates the voices of students who do not have the maturity to appropriately censor themselves. Racist, sexist, and other blatantly inappropriate comments that are made through various media must be dealt with directly. These types of serious indiscretions have been so few and far between that they are barely an issue to be concerned with in my experience.

Yes, some students post silly comments, but the most surprising development I have repeatedly witnessed is how students are often disciplined by their classmates who call them out respectfully and, in turn, keep the conversations focused and aboveboard. In cases where authoritative intervention is needed to offset these comments in the during-class twitter stream, I have found that the most effective strategy has been to make a quick passing comment aloud that acknowledges the tweet and calls attention to its inanity. I have found it particularly effective to do so in a humorous and self-effacing way in order to insert a bit of levity into the proceedings; such levity can diffuse the disruptive potential of the inappropriate tweet.

Technology Integration Unsettles Classroom Routine. Several of the strategies that I describe elicited initial fear, uncertainty, and a sense of diminished control as the authority in the classroom. These initial negative feelings have been more than offset by the positive outcomes. Still, the types of technology integration that I have suggested can be awkward at first for both professors and students.

NEW DIRECTIONS FOR TEACHING AND LEARNING • DOI: 10.1002/tl

Professors must learn new ways of leading a course. They must subtly manage how the conversation unfolds, remaining ever flexible to follow a productive tangent or digression that might emerge in the during-class tweet stream or on the course Facebook page. To be sure, one must be nimble as a reactive moderator, drawing links and connections between what is happening in class and virtually while thinking on one's feet. This is difficult and can be unsettling if professors cannot find comfort in their new, organic role.

More important than obsessing over our own sense of being unsettled because of social media integration strategies, professors should celebrate, not bemoan, the unsettling that is happening for students. We are unsettling students' commonly accepted passive stance in the classroom. The hum of multitasking is matched by the eyes of students following the bustle of classroom articulations and ideas. They are out of their comfort zones and unsettled, but giving Millennial students a voice in the large class proceedings serves to encourage a vitality that often is not found in the large lecture hall.

Focus on Technology Undermines Course Content. Some want to argue that by putting emphasis on the tools being used, we are detracting from the robustness of the content. This argument further extends to suggest that the use of these tools in the classroom panders to students' egos, coddling their attention deficits with solutions that debase serious educational intentions. We cannot overlook, however, that we live in a time when new media are an intrinsic part of student life; and while the dynamic of interpersonal communication is certainly changing (Baron 2008), Baym (2010) reminds us that it is counterproductive to rush to judgment in assessing what these changes to the communicative landscape actually mean. It is a fact that we live in a wired (or wireless) world of instant information that at times, like the Greek sirens, beckons us almost irresistibly to detrimental ends. It is also a fact that we have never had greater capability to share information and communicate interpersonally with more people in more ways on more levels. These information and communication potentials connect all classroom participants to the world beyond the professor's viewpoint; they also connect Millennial students more viscerally to each other as a learning community. Collectively, then, the types of technology integration that I have described support the purposes of education.

Conclusion

Good teaching has always been an iterative process of continually learning, changing tactics, and taking risks. When done with sensitivity, substantial detailed forethought, and constant critical reflexivity, professors can radically transform the large lecture hall by harnessing the power of "disruptive" technologies in ways that not only elevate student presence and participation but also reconceptualize the educational process by supporting Millennial students' visceral connections between subject matter and their sense of self. By using social media to implicitly position every participant as an agent in learning that is simultaneously interesting, relevant, pertinent, unpredictable, uncertain, challenging, risky, illuminating, and even frustrating at times, we foster spaces for learning that are more intimate, inviting, and meaningful.

Ultimately, the approaches described in this chapter are productive inasmuch as they do not reproduce tested educational tropes. Hitching our pedagogical designs to structures that are tailored to student proclivities and that invite wider participation of their voices can actually serve to inspire them to engage their learning on the terms we both mutually seek. In short, it is a compromise not in the sense of a reducing, weakening, or lowering of the quality and value of their education, but in the sense of constituting meaningful practices that combine the qualities of mobile devices and social media to become more effective in the complex mission of education. In doing so, we channel Millennial students' egos into the learning process to augment, rather than constrain, outcomes.

References

Baron, N. 2008. *Always On: Language in an Online and Mobile World*. New York: Oxford University Press.

Baym, N. 2010. *Personal Connections in the Digital Age*. Cambridge, UK: Polity Press.

Elavsky, C. M. 2012. "You Can't Go Back Now: Incorporating 'Disruptive' Technologies in the Large Lecture Hall." In *Social Media: Usage and Impact*, edited by H. Noor Al-deen and J. Hendricks, 75–92. Lanham, MD: Lexington Books.

Elavsky, C. M., C. Mislan, and S. Elavsky. 2011. "When Talking Less Is More: Exploring Outcomes of Twitter Usage in the Large-Lecture Hall." *Learning, Media and Technology* 36 (3): 215–233.

Knowlton, D. S. 2004. "Electronic Bulletin Boards as Medium for Asynchronous Problem Solving in Field Experiences." *International Journal of Instructional Technology & Distance Education* 1 (5): 43–52. Accessed October 10, 2012. http://itdl .org/Journal/May_04/article06.htm.

Knowlton, D. S. 2010. "Take Out the Tests, and Hide the Grades; Add the Spiritual with All Voices Raised! Professor Explications and Students' Opinions of an Unconventional Classroom Milieu." *Critical Questions in Education* 1 (2): 70–93. Accessed October 15, 2012. http://education.missouristate.edu/AcadEd/87193 .htm.

Matheson, R., S. C. Wilkinson, and E. Gilhooly. 2012. "Promoting Critical Thinking and Collaborative Working through Assessment: Combining Patchwork Text and Online Discussion Boards." *Innovations in Education and Teaching International* 49 (3): 257–267.

Rochman, B. 2009. "Twittering in Church, with the Pastor's OK." *Time*, May 3. www .time.com/time/magazine/article/0,9171,1900265,00.htm.

Rollag, K. 2010. "Teaching Business Cases Online through Discussion Boards: Strategies and Best Practices." *Journal of Management Education* 34 (4): 499–526.

C. MICHAEL ELAVSKY *is associate professor in the Department of Media Studies at the Pennsylvania State University.*

9

This chapter discusses the opportunities created by out-of-class interactions. These interactions allow for ego-engaged exchanges between students and professors.

Affirming Ego through Out-of-Class Interactions: A Practitioner's View

Heather M. Knowlton

Out-of-class interactions between professors and students can "have a significant impact" (Cotton and Wilson 2006, 488). For example, out-of-class interactions can be therapeutic because they serve as a way for professors and students to get to know each other interpersonally and informally, which can help students relax and feel less tense than they do in the more formal setting of the classroom. Also, through out-of-class interactions, the student and professor can examine the goings-on within the classroom, which can deepen student learning regarding course content and help students think about themselves and their own learning in more personal ways than during-class activities allow. All of this can heighten students' sense of ownership, power, and ego-driven involvement. Students routinely do not achieve this level during formal class settings (Cox 2009). Why not? Within formal classroom structures, assessment standards and classroom norms are not tailored to the individual student's needs. A recent article points out that students see the benefits of interacting with professors outside of class. In that article, one student remarked, "[I] responded better to professors who interacted with me outside of class" (Bowen et al. 2011, 29).

In spite of these benefits, out-of-class interactions are difficult because they can be an emotional grab bag—volatile and unpredictable. You never know what you will get. For example, professors often perceive students as approaching them with a sense of arrogance, entitlement, and grandiosity; and sometimes they are doing so. Our natural response as professors

NEW DIRECTIONS FOR TEACHING AND LEARNING, no. 135, Fall 2013 © Wiley Periodicals, Inc.
Published online in Wiley Online Library (wileyonlinelibrary.com) • DOI: 10.1002/tl.20067

may be to assert our own authority and dominance. After all, we are the *professor*—with degrees, wisdom, knowledge, and experience. Surely, we should not be expected to pacify and endure the emotional flux of the Millennial student. Should we?

From my perspective, the increased desire to embody authority and dominance stems from my physicality. As a petite, white female who stands at 5 feet 3½ inches—and takes great pride in that extra ½ inch—I want to stand my ground and be in charge. Based on my experience teaching first-year college students in both university and community college settings, however, I have found that if I shift my perspective and see students' emotions as ones that they do not know how to deal with, then I can respond with compassion, kindness, and gentleness in order to help mitigate both my own perceptions and student emotions. When we change our approach to problematic situations, the problematic situations tend to wane (Dyer 2006). In interacting with students outside of class, I have found this change in approach to be particularly useful.

The rest of this chapter is organized around practical advice that might help create productively softer out-of-class interactions with students. In many cases, a professor's approach can compel students to give their own voices to problems and issues. In other cases, the professor's voice can be used to model ideas for students. In both cases, professors must risk vulnerability with students if they are to gain ego involvement in their course from those students.

Come Early; Stay Late; Hear Their Voice

Contrast the physical and psychological space of during-class sessions with the same dimensions of space before and after class. During class, the space is large, crowded, and formal; professor and student are separated by a podium, desktops, and competing needs and demands of students. Before and after class, however, that space is smaller and more intimate. In this space, professors and students can chat face-to-face. Such informal chats allow students to share themselves more authentically.

Just from the act of arriving early, showing interest in students' lives, and hearing their voices, I have discovered and learned from amateur songwriters, home improvement specialists, athletic superstars, and budding entrepreneurs. Millennial students have considerable expertise that they have developed in their lives, and I find the moments before and after class to be a useful time of engagement to learn about that expertise. Through this engagement, we validate them as people, not simply as students. We may be among the first adults outside of their families to do so.

It is amazing to me, particularly in the community college, how many times even Millennial students describe their education as "their time." They have already devoted their short lives to military service, aging parents, ever-mounting debt, and other life circumstances. And now with those circumstances changed, it is "their time" to achieve something personally meaningful and fulfilling. And to think, if I did not arrive early and stay late, I would miss the opportunity to hear their authentic voice and, instead, only know students as "that C student on the back row" or "the one who doesn't understand apostrophes."

Be Still and Use Silence

After one class session, a student and I walked out together: "I'm not worried about doing well in this class. I know how to bullshit my way through any project." I stopped. She stopped, too. I kept eye contact with her but remained silent. She began speaking again: "I did find that Katelynn had some helpful advice during today's peer editing. I like her idea of using a personal example in my introduction."

Being still and using silence can create psychological space for students to gain sudden insight and make connections. During hushed moments, students have nowhere else to go but within. And it is from within that deep learning occurs. All of us have had that moment where we pause mentally (and even physically) to think and find our answer. Silence can be very powerful when used in response to student arrogance because "stillness fosters awareness" (*The Book of Yoga* 2010, 8). Using stillness as a response to students' comments opens their minds because "we're far more inspiring to others when we're willing to listen than when we're giving advice" (Dyer 2006, 149). When professors are silent, they help students understand how to listen to themselves. Certainly, stillness and silence can be used during class, but because of the intimacy of out-of-class interaction, stillness and silence can have an even more dramatic effect.

Promote Depth in Students' Voice

The previous example deals with helping students hear and recognize their own voice. But because of the intimacy of out-of-class interactions, professors can help students develop depth in their own voice through careful interactions with them.

After class, a student asked, "Is this a good introduction and thesis for my paper?" From his question, I inferred that he either didn't understand or didn't value a key course concept—that all good ideas emerge from the process of writing to discover what one has to say.

"What do you discuss in the body of your paper?"

"I haven't written the body yet. I'm on the introduction."

His answer helped me further diagnose that he was not connecting course content with his own work: "What do you remember about the reading and discussion we had a week ago about drafting your paper?"

"I think that section said that we have to discover what we want to say, and we talked about that you have to write and revise to discover what you want to say."

"What do you want to say in your paper?"

"I'm not sure. I guess I need to do some drafting." He paused for a moment. "I get it! I've been doing this backwards!"

I inferred from his body language and tone of voice that this was a meaningful moment of insight for this student. This anecdote provides a classic case of allowing a student to explain to himself what he did not know that he knew. By prompting the student to give the answer in his own voice, this out-of-class interaction allowed course content to become more authentic. This exchange could not have been conducted during class; both time constraints and the very publicness of the setting likely would have stifled the student's breakthrough realization.

On the surface, it may seem as if I simply reviewed lecture notes with the student, allowing him to do nothing more than cater to *my* voice as previously presented during class lectures. But notice that I provided no information about course content during this interaction. I only prompted his understanding with questions. By paraphrasing the course content and thus making connections for himself, this out-of-class interaction provided him with an opportunity to express a more applied understanding of course content. He expressed it for himself—in his own voice, with his own words. A student's own words are indicative of that student's personalized language and thus the student's own thinking (Sharp, Knowlton, and Weiss 2005).

Certainly, though, we can help students through out-of-class conversation to deepen their voice in ways other than urging for paraphrase. During out-of-class meetings, I have had opportunities to prompt students to connect their own hobbies, jobs, and personal interests to course content. Even in a simple out-of-class discussion about a television commercial, one student found his voice for connecting elements of advertising with literary analysis. Professors should help students relate course material to their lives outside the classroom (Bowen et al. 2011). Because out-of-class interactions allow for customized discussion that targets an individual student's needs, professors can use these interactions to deepen a student's voice in ways that are not possible during formal class sessions.

Show Compassion While Promoting Accountability

"I know that you say you do not take journals late, but I've been sick all night and this morning. I could only get an appointment with my doctor during your class today. Would you accept my journal next week?"

It's a typical e-mail from a student, isn't it? Excuse after excuse; as professors we have heard it all: from the heroic ("I saved my neighbor's life") to the everyday ("I overslept") and including the odd ("I had water at the end of my driveway, and I don't drive when it's wet"). Students often share their excuses, obstacles, struggles, and sense of defeat, all of which, they believe, are holding them back in the course or even in life.

NEW DIRECTIONS FOR TEACHING AND LEARNING • DOI: 10.1002/tl

I must confess that my own level of sympathy for such matters is low. When I was a freshman in college, my house burned down the week before Thanksgiving, and I still was able to turn in all my assignments on time, and I did not miss a single class. Those who, like me, were engaged at an ego level in their own education would not think of using trials and challenges as reasons for missing class or submitting work late. Such people— and I would suspect that many professors fall into this category—would see it as a personal defeat to succumb to setbacks.

But, when students approach us out of class with their own trials, we should see an opportunity to connect compassionately with the student: "First, the important stuff. It's awful to be sick in the middle of a busy semester. I know firsthand. I hope everything is all right and that you are doing well."

Offering a compassionate response to students does not mean that we are pushovers. In fact, we should hold them accountable and help them see that policies are in place to promote fairness and accountability: "Second, the answer to your question: You can e-mail your journal to me by midnight tonight, and I will count it as on time. After midnight, I can't take it. In order to be fair to those who have turned in their work on time, I must stick to my policies as defined in the syllabus."

I ended my e-mail, though, with additional assurances that more opportunities exist in the future, and she will be able to take advantage of those opportunities: "Remember, this is only one lost opportunity in this course. You will have more journals that you can submit on time. This will help your grade and, more importantly, help your learning."

E-mail exchanges take place in a different space from both out-of-class face-to-face discussions and during-class activities. When responding to students' e-mails or other digital exchanges, we must learn to work without the benefit of interpersonal cues, and we must understand that students imagine a negative tone of voice within professors' e-mail communications. Because of these potential pitfalls in meaningful e-mail communication, I was delighted to receive an optimistic reply from the student: "Thanks for your reply. The truth is, as I was writing my e-mail to you, I knew what your answer would be, but I guess I needed to ask and hear that everything would be okay. See you next week."

At times, students only want reassurance from their professors (Cox 2009); and by sandwiching accountability between compassion and hope we can give that reassurance in productive ways. My experiences suggest that students are more inclined to receive the balance of compassion and accountability in out-of-class interactions than they are while reading a formal policy manifesto delivered through a syllabus.

Conclusion

Out-of-class interactions are not just additional instructional time. They are unique opportunities to move toward students—to get inside their ego

NEW DIRECTIONS FOR TEACHING AND LEARNING • DOI: 10.1002/tl

circle in ways not possible during class. The examples in this chapter illustrate possibilities and can serve as a reminder. Out-of-class interactions have a unique power to lead students to understand who they are as learners and, more important, as human beings. This unique understanding of self is realized when professors help Millennial students learn how to share and deepen their own voices through interaction with professors. Because of the unique educational leverage of out-of-class interactions, professors should look for ways to make them happen.

References

The Book of Yoga, rev. ed. 2010. Bath, UK: Parragon.

Bowen, G., C. Burton, C. Cooper, L. Cruz, A. McFadden, C. Reich, and M. Wargo. 2011. "Listening to the Voices of Today's Undergraduates: Implications for Teaching and Learning." *Journal of the Scholarship of Teaching and Learning* 11 (3): 21–33.

Cotton, S., and B. Wilson. 2006. "Student-Faculty Interactions: Dynamics and Determinants." *Higher Education* 51 (4): 487–519. doi:10.1007/s10734-004-1705-4.

Cox, R. 2009. *The College Fear Factor*. Cambridge, MA: Harvard University Press.

Dyer, W. 2006. *Inspiration: Your Ultimate Calling*. Carlsbad, CA: Hay House.

Sharp, D. C., D. S. Knowlton, and R. E. Weiss. 2005. "Applications of Generative Learning for the Survey of International Economics Course." *Journal of Economic Education* 36 (4): 345–357.

HEATHER M. KNOWLTON is an adjunct English instructor at both Lewis & Clark Community College and Southern Illinois University Edwardsville.

10

This chapter argues that the affirmation of Millennial students' egos is an essential aspect of a social justice curriculum.

Engaging Millennial Students in Social Justice from Initial Class Meetings to Service Learning

Jonathan J. Cavallero

Despite a preponderance of media attention, a committed fan base, seven Grammys, and over 20 million record sales worldwide, it seems that John Mayer is waiting. Purporting to speak for his generation, Mayer tells us in "Waiting on the World to Change" (2006) that he and other people his age see the problems that the world faces but that "we just feel like we don't have the means to rise above and beat it." It is an odd statement coming from a commercially successful and critically acclaimed artist who has the far-reaching power of media conglomerates at his back, and yet Mayer's sentiment is widely felt and often expressed among undergraduates these days. It is not that they do not see injustice; it is that they feel powerless to change it.

A curriculum focused on social justice issues can help students to recognize inequalities and develop the confidence to work toward a more equitable world. Defining *social justice* is a difficult task, but there is general agreement that it centers on "notions of equity or alleviating disparity and the redistribution of resources" (Miller et al. 2009, 495). Advocates recognize that there are "structural and institutional inequities," and that they often center around "categories, such as gender, race/ethnicity, class, disability, age, and sexual orientation" (Prentice 2007, 266). Drawing attention to social justice issues, and cultivating a sense of agency, responsibility, and possibility in students, is a moral obligation for all professors. But the

NEW DIRECTIONS FOR TEACHING AND LEARNING, no. 135, Fall 2013 © Wiley Periodicals, Inc.
Published online in Wiley Online Library (wileyonlinelibrary.com) • DOI: 10.1002/tl.20068

goals of social justice seem antithetical to a teaching style that affirms Millennial students' egos. One seems to focus students on themselves, and the other looks to inequalities in local and global communities of which the self may have little or no experience. However, it is precisely the affirmation of ego that allows students to believe in themselves and the efficacy of their actions; and when students become more culturally aware, they often gain a perspective that empowers them to act.

Building Trust during Initial Class Meetings

Put simply, in my film studies courses, I seek to enact a curriculum that first recognizes that inequalities exist and then works to correct (or at least alleviate some of) them. For me, this process rests on the establishment of a safe environment where students feel comfortable discussing and confronting their own identities. And so, I work to earn my students' trust by expressing an interest in them as individuals. The better I can understand them, their views, and their backgrounds, the better I can mold my teaching to meet them where they are. But, as bell hooks (1994, 21) writes, "Professors who expect students to share confessional narratives but who are themselves unwilling to share are exercising power in a manner that could be coercive."

In an effort to level the playing field, I begin each semester with a discussion of my teaching philosophy during which I highlight some of the personal experiences that have helped to shape that philosophy. For example, a few weeks into my first-ever teaching assignment, several of my best students asked if I could make my lecture notes available before class. The students felt that having the notes would allow them to focus more on the lecture and ultimately glean more information from the class. After considering the situation, I denied the request but struggled to find the reasoning for my decision. Both of my parents have teaching experience, and when I spoke with them about it, my father said, "If you are doing your job correctly, some of the most important things students will learn in your class will have nothing to do with the movies." Among these are note-taking and listening skills, which students will use even if they never embark on a career in filmmaking. Acknowledging this decision process works to build trust between my students and me by conveying that course policies are not arbitrary but rather have been established with the hope of providing the best possible educational experience.

During initial course meetings, I also build trust as I discuss course content. I tell my students that there is no such thing as an objective course since each teacher makes decisions about what to include and what to exclude. Rather than being neutral choices, these decisions have a bearing on the way we understand the subject. This move acknowledges my own power in framing the course topic, and I hope it makes my students feel that they can take issue with opinions that are offered from the front of the classroom. They need to see me not as someone who has all the answers (obviously, I don't) but rather as an individual who struggles with many of the same issues that they confront as citizens and consumers.

All of these strategies expose my privileges as a professor, which is crucial to gaining students' trust and allowing them to acknowledge (rather than deny) their own prejudices. After all, the point here is not to prove my own worth as an individual but rather to build an environment where students feel comfortable seeing and understanding themselves, acknowledging their own privileges, and moving toward a greater sense of self-actualization. Admittedly, these strategies that I use in initial class meetings are far removed from the kind of social justice pedagogy to which I aspire, but developing an effective social justice curriculum takes time, and professors need to be patient (Landreman et al. 2008).

Personalizing Unproductive Attitudes and Expectations

As the semester progresses, my personal stories become more intimate, sometimes emphasizing self-criticism. I tell my students about an experience I had when I was 15 years old, and a group of men that I assumed were gay sat next to me while I watched a musical play with my family. I was so uncomfortable that I switched seats with one of my parents during the intermission. I tell my students how ashamed I feel about that incident, and I ask them where my assumptions about gay people might have originated since I did not know any openly gay individuals at the time. My students are usually quick to realize that I identified these men as gay because they conformed to a series of stereotypes that I had learned, at least in part, from the media. Indeed, growing up in the 1980s, I saw plenty of programs and newscasts that represented gay men as diseased.

That certainly does not forgive my actions, but it helps to explain my thoughts at the time while highlighting the power that the media have to define groups of people. Since many of my students aspire to careers in media production or journalism, I use this moment to highlight the social responsibility they assume when they enter such professions. Whether they like it or not, the stories they write and the works they create will help to define groups of people for at least some of their audience. But even if they don't aspire to such careers, my hope is that this discussion highlights the ways in which different groups are treated unfairly by cultural institutions and how that treatment manifests itself in individuals' attitudes and expectations.

Combatting Cynicism and Building Student Confidence

Once students recognize their cultural roles, I try to build their confidence and encourage a sense of agency—both of which are crucial to any social

New Directions for Teaching and Learning • DOI: 10.1002/tl

justice initiative. As Miller et al. (2009) write, "It is possible that self-efficacy might be related to a sense of empowerment, which is essential for facilitating social justice advocacy" (496). In film and television studies, this can be especially difficult since a critical perspective toward media so often entails the recognition of the cultural power that media industries exercise over individuals, their perceived choices, and their desires. Part of my job is to temper a student's uncritical love of film and TV by encouraging a more informed viewership and more educated media consumption. This can breed cynicism because students begin to recognize that a few corporations control the vast majority of media and that the economic system of Hollywood tends to reward productions that ignore or soften controversial political topics. As Ray (1985) and Tomasulo (1990) have shown, movies try to appeal to as many sides of the political spectrum as possible in order to attract a mass audience. Students can begin to feel cynical toward Hollywood and duped since their previous passion for film seems naive.

As a graduate student at Indiana University, I learned an important lesson from one of my mentors, Ted Striphas: One way to restore student self-confidence is to frame students not just as media consumers but also as media producers. Creating a Facebook page, assembling an iTunes playlist, or shooting a short video are all ways that students produce original media content. Further, their ability to reach an audience is greatly enhanced by the technology at their disposal and their generation's familiarity with it. Today, students can shoot a video with their cell phones, edit that video on their laptops, and post it to YouTube, Facebook, or any number of other sites where a large audience may access it. This offers students a powerful way to distribute their message, and it has the potential to influence on a level that I never could have imagined when I was taking video production classes in the 1990s. For me, shooting a video meant signing out equipment, traveling to the editing room, and then physically taking the VHS tape to any viewers who were willing to watch it.

I also try to build a sense of agency by highlighting the ways in which the culture has already changed and the role my students have played in changing it. For example, I ask my students to raise their hands if they went to a high school where at least one student was "out" as gay, lesbian, or bisexual. I have asked that question in Indiana, Pennsylvania, and Arkansas in courses that varied in size from about 20 to over 500, and the vast majority of students in each class have raised their hands. I applaud my students for that progress since it would have been unthinkable for anyone in my upper-middle-class, suburban Philadelphia high school to come out in the early 1990s. The culture has become more accepting of sexual diversity, and many of my students have helped to forge that progress. In drawing this to their attention, I hope to convey a sense of possibility when it comes to cultural change.

Empowering Students with Service-Learning Projects

Service learning "combines academic study with community service" and "is ideally suited to achieving both the personal and academic goals of students and the broader goals of civic responsibility and social justice" (Ngai 2006, 165). My most successful social justice initiatives have been service-learning projects. In 2011, I was teaching an international film course. In March of that year, when an earthquake and tsunami devastated Japan, I decided to offer interested students an alternative to my standard research paper assignment; this alternative would require research and writing comparable to the research paper, but it provided the opportunity for students to design and enact a service-learning initiative. About half of my students, 12 in all, chose to participate.

The alternate assignment consisted of four one-page journal entries. The first required students to watch a Japanese film of their choosing and write a reaction to it. The second required students to research the effects of the disasters in Japan and write about the economic, environmental, and human impacts. The third, due only a few weeks before the end of the semester, took the form of a proposal that outlined the actions that the group could take to make a difference in the relief efforts. After reading the proposals, I nominated four, and then the students voted for the idea that they thought would have the greatest impact and on which they would enjoy working. The fourth journal entry, due after the completion of the project, provided an opportunity for students to reflect on their involvement and sift through the lessons they learned. My hope was that these journals created a progression for students from developing a deeper sense of cultural awareness to realizing that individuals had the power to make a difference in the world and culminating in recognizing their growth as individuals.

One student was an employee at a local restaurant that was part of a national chain. He was able to arrange a fund-raiser where a percentage of the night's sales would be donated to Japanese relief efforts. Students supported the project by undertaking individual tasks that best fit their strengths. Some students designed and distributed flyers that advertised the event. Others solicited donations from area businesses for a raffle. A few liaised with the Japanese Student Association and the Panhellenic Council to draw attention to the fund-raiser. Still others "chalked" sidewalks, created a Facebook group, and listed the information on the university newswire service. A few even folded origami cranes at the restaurant since Japanese legend holds that if an individual folds 1,000 origami cranes the person's wish will come true.

The project raised over $320, built cultural awareness by exposing students to the films of another country, enhanced students' global knowledge, encouraged them to think about the challenges that others faced, promoted a sense of teamwork, and encouraged students to see themselves

New Directions for Teaching and Learning • DOI: 10.1002/tl

as difference makers who were not powerless. As one student wrote in her final journal entry,

> The money was not the most important part of it for me. I learned that people can change the lives of others, even ones all the way across the world. I was very involved in my own life and did not even think it was possible for me to help, but this experience showed me that it is possible, and also very enjoyable. It was a labor of love to know that the work you are doing is not just for a grade; it is for the good of another human being, and that was just awesome.

Conclusion

Confronting social justice issues in the classroom can be uncomfortable, and there are those who would rather not tackle such controversial topics. But ignoring instances of inequality perpetuates injustice and makes the problem exponentially worse. It suggests that ignorance and complacency are the ways to confront unfairness and offers the impression that individuals are powerless to effect positive change. The international film students discussed in this chapter came to see the world in a different way—a way that affirmed their egos and framed them as actors who could create a better world. Rather than waiting on the world to change, they helped to change it.

References

hooks, b. 1994. *Teaching to Transgress: Education as the Practice of Freedom.* New York: Routledge.

Landreman, L., K. E. Edwards, D. Garma Balón, and G. Anderson. 2008. "Wait! It Takes Time to Develop Rich and Relevant Social Justice Curriculum." *About Campus* 13 (4): 2–10.

Mayer, J. 2006. "Waiting on the World to Change." On *Continuum* [CD]. Evanston, IL: Aware Records.

Miller, M. J., K. Sendrowitz, C. Connacher, S. Blanco, C. Muñiz de la Peña, S. Bernardi, and L. Morere. 2009. "College Students' Social Justice Interest and Commitment: A Social-Cognitive Perspective." *Journal of Counseling Psychology* 56: 495–507.

Ngai, S. 2006. "Service-Learning, Personal Development, and Social Commitment: A Case Study of University Students in Hong Kong." *Adolescence* 41 (161): 165–176.

Prentice, M. 2007. "Social Justice through Service Learning: Community Colleges as Ground Zero." *Equity & Excellence in Education* 40 (3): 266–273.

Ray, R. 1985. *A Certain Tendency of the Hollywood Cinema, 1930–1980.* Princeton, NJ: Princeton University Press.

Tomasulo, F. P. 1990. "The Politics of Ambivalence: *Apocalypse Now* as Postwar and Antiwar Film." In *From Hanoi to Hollywood: The Vietnam War in American Film*, edited by L. Dittmar and G. Michaud, 145–158. New Brunswick, NJ: Rutgers University Press.

Jonathan J. Cavallero is an assistant professor of rhetoric at Bates College in Lewiston, Maine.

11

Working with a model of students as citizens rather than consumers, this chapter focuses on assessment and evaluation as tools to motivate self-directed learning.

From Consumers to Citizens: Student-Directed Goal Setting and Assessment

David R. Coon, Ingrid Walker

In his 2012 State of the Union address, President Obama declared, "Higher education can't be a luxury—it is an economic imperative." This notion of higher education as an economic necessity reminds us why many of our students are in college: to get a degree that will lead to a better job. Students' focus on the outcome of education is often evident through their investment in individual courses; they focus almost entirely on the end point—their grade—rather than on the learning process.

Traditional assessment practices often reinforce this focus. After all, most higher education institutions require professors to quantify student performance. Sometimes professors are required to align those quantifications with formal and official outcomes. These conventions establish a power dynamic that poses a challenge to student-directed learning. Students must disregard their own goals in order to achieve preapproved course outcomes, outcomes from which students often feel completely disconnected. These conventions also lead students to deduce that any liberties that professors may encourage them to take pose a risk to their end goal of passing the class with a strong grade. Even the best intentions of professors to neutralize the tendency for students to seek out "what the professor wants," and to encourage them to become members of a learning community by engaging with meaningful challenges for the sake of learning, are doomed.

New Directions for Teaching and Learning, no. 135, Fall 2013 © Wiley Periodicals, Inc.
Published online in Wiley Online Library (wileyonlinelibrary.com) • DOI: 10.1002/tl.20069

One practice through which students come to see and claim their learning, thereby engaging their egos in the learning process, is the assessment of their own and others' performance. While recognizing that assessment can be fraught with challenges and limitations for both faculty and students, we believe it is key to engaging students' egos and fostering educational citizenship. In this chapter, we begin with a short explanation of citizenship and its connection to assessment. Then, we offer numerous strategies for activating citizenship within assessment and evaluation practices. Those strategies include facilitating student goal setting, scaffolding discrete learning skills, allowing for assessment by external stakeholders, and implementing course critiques.

Citizenship and the Importance of Authentic Assessment

At its core, citizenship signifies "belonging to and participation in a group or community—something that brings with it certain rights and obligations" (Plummer 2003, 50). When they act as educational citizens, students adopt productive views of both rights and obligations. As citizens, students have the right to access the resources that define the learning community, which include the knowledge and experience of professors, fellow students, and external stakeholders. Students also have an obligation to engage actively with those resources and to generate their own contributions that improve and expand the learning community.

Given the importance of these rights and responsibilities, a professor's initial concern in working with students may be facilitating a perspective shift from the educational consumer who pays for an education and expects a door-opening degree to the educational citizen who joins a community of learners and takes an active, intentional role in learning. If professors wish to engage students intrinsically in their educations, they might start by recognizing that most students will not become permanent citizens of the university, and thus those professors must consider what citizenship could mean for students during their short stay and what it could mean to the rest of their lives.

Mentoring students by encouraging connections between their goal of passing the course and meaningful learning goals helps frame self-directed learning. To do that in a purposeful way requires professors to engage students by inviting the ego and encouraging them to imagine beyond the immediate goal of "getting through a class." Boud and Falchikov (2007, 186) argue that for students to succeed in applied future learning, they must first identify themselves as *active learners* and then recognize their own levels of knowledge as well as gaps in their knowledge. We have found that effective assessment practices can help students use what they do know to identify what they do not yet know. This supports students in active and self-directed learning, engaging the ego by enabling them to use existing skills while identifying gaps in their knowledge. We see this as a

NEW DIRECTIONS FOR TEACHING AND LEARNING • DOI: 10.1002/tl

form of university citizenship that encourages students to exercise their rights as agents in their education.

While we encourage the use of assessment procedures that engage students' egos, we also are aware that some students' egos may be fragile, and professors often overlook the emotional impact of the assessment process (Clegg and Bryan 2006; Falchikov and Boud 2007). For students new to college and its conventions, there can be a tendency to conflate task with ego, so that a failing grade may suggest to students that they *are* failures rather than that they have failed at a task. Moving to transparent, process-based assessments and evaluation can help students see that failing is an essential part of the learning experience (Clegg and Bryan 2006). Giving students permission, the opportunity, and space to fail and try again can be necessary to their ability to break through the "please the teacher" mode and become educational citizens.

Student Goal Setting

Educational citizenship requires that student learning is in some ways self-determined; that is, students must have the right to exercise some authority over the establishment of goals and learning outcomes. Tan (2007, 119) writes that what engages students' egos is "future-driven assessment," which has the power to sustain itself beyond a class or program of study because it connects performance and achievement in the present to goals for the future. Professors can work to align student preconceptions and desires with faculty expectations and course goals (Cox 2009). As professors do so, students see the assessment of their current performance both as a step toward their professional and personal future and as part of a context of broader academic learning. Specifically, it can help students envision how multidisciplinary skills and knowledge have application elsewhere.

At the beginning of the term, we ask students to set two or three goals related to what they hope to learn or accomplish in the class. Some students set goals related to content or knowledge acquisition, whereas others focus on improving skills such as writing or public speaking. Students explain how their goals will help them to progress toward their future personal, professional, or academic goals.

Some students need help articulating their goals or making realistic connections between course work and life goals. For example, students in an introductory computer programming class might need help understanding how much progress they can reasonably expect to make in a single term. Students in a literature course might not immediately see the long-term value of close textual analysis. If, however, a professor explains that textual analysis can enhance a student's eye for detail and that attention to detail is a skill with applications well beyond literature, then students are more likely to successfully connect present learning with future goals. Once students make these connections, they not only are more likely to

NEW DIRECTIONS FOR TEACHING AND LEARNING • DOI: 10.1002/tl

recognize the gaps between their current performance and their desired performance, but also they seem more inclined to view constructive criticism as a helpful tool for future growth rather than as an indictment of them as a person.

Scaffolding Discrete Skills

Most students do not arrive at college with a strong skill set in self-assessment and self-evaluation. Such skills need to be scaffolded and developed. There is an interesting allegory here between students' assessment skills and skateboarding. When attempting complex tricks, novice, intermediate, and expert skaters all wipe out far more often than they land (10 : 1 ratio). Why is this true? When we asked one organizer of skateboarding events, we received an interesting answer: "It's simple. Everyone can see when you're not trying hard enough."

Because the challenge to master new skills is the main currency in skating, skaters tend not to respect those who do not attempt a new level of difficulty or mastery on every turn. Professors have a similar experience—we know immediately when our students are not challenging themselves. It is more difficult for students to see this as readily as do both professors and skaters and, once they do see it, to feel emboldened to attempt and risk more.

We show our students a slow-motion video of skaters wiping out. Students immediately realize that a skater has successfully executed several of the skills required in a difficult trick but has not achieved the entire sequence. This depicts so clearly that "falling off the skateboard" is not failure; it is one part of a complex act. To be fully successful, students conclude, one must master the multiple elements inherent in any task, but mastering those elements necessarily requires failing at some of them as one learns.

To build upon this initial lesson, we have found value in rubrics or metrics that make visible the alignment between various elements in an assignment and the skill-based competencies that students must develop to achieve those elements. This type of alignment gives students a clear road map for developing their skills. This approach flourished for us when we connected all the dots within a course: scaffolding discrete skills from simpler assignments through to culminating complex assignments with a single rubric to build a set of skills across the term. Practicing and applying skills in a variety of smaller assignments helped students see them more clearly when they were combined in a final assignment. Students self- and peer-reviewed during various stages of the assignments and received professor assessments on the same rubric. This allowed students to align various assessments, recognizing where they successfully acquired knowledge or completed skills and identifying those yet to be mastered. This process helped students to see themselves as citizens who had rights in and obligations to the practitioner-driven community of which they were a part.

Assessment by External Stakeholders

Including an external perspective can validate and round out students' sense of themselves as practitioners. Assessment by outside stakeholders, particularly those who work in fields that will eventually employ our graduates, can be powerful in engaging students' egos while broadening notions of citizenship. While not appropriate in all classes, many classes in which students produce reports, projects, or presentations that model the work they will produce after graduation provide unique opportunity for external assessment. In our classes, we have invited various professionals to engage our students in evaluation. Professional writers and artists have conducted critiques of student work in class. The opportunity to have external review of authentic work can be particularly valuable in modeling real-world evaluative practices. For example, a local business owner may assess the merits of students' marketing plans, or directors of local nonprofit organizations might provide students with evaluations of simulated grant proposals.

Course Critique as Opportunity for Reflection

Professors can engage students' egos by informally inviting student input about a class session's successes and weaknesses. Once professors make course corrections based on that input, they can further engage students' egos by inviting reactions to those corrections. Midterm surveys, group critiques, and soliciting feedback from students about the learning value of assignments all give students the right to inform change in the learning environment. These processes lay the foundation for a high-impact, formal classroom practice: the class critique. At midterm and at term's end, the professor can lead students in a set of conversations about the class structure, content, instruction, and student contributions. At midterm, class critiques not only allow students to inform professors about confusions, but also they demonstrate that evaluation is a process that can inform assessment of learning. Through class critiques conducted at midterm, professors can gain an even better understanding of students' goals and how those goals relate to official course goals. In turn, professors can use that information to recalibrate their lesson plans to better ensure their contribution to student success.

At the end of the term, students are better situated to review their evaluative efforts. In our courses, students tend to have spirited discussions about why various elements of the course did or did not work well to support the course goals. Where some would remove a reading, others argue for its retention and cite evidence to connect it to important learning outcomes. Student citizens not only operationalize the course's learning objectives, but also articulate its logic and outcomes. Frequently, students have said this is when the class really came together for them, where they acted and engaged others as practitioners, taking into account all learning experiences. Through this process of engaging others, many students have novel realizations about the course, their performance, and their role as educational citizens.

Authentic self-evaluation in the classroom requires us as faculty to participate in and model the practice of assessing our work. Making transparent our own informal self-evaluation as professors helps students understand that we continually perform the self-reflection that we require of them. Sharing our developmental processes in instruction and curriculum design—both successes and "falls off our skateboard"—builds credibility with students and equity in classroom evaluation.

The more intentional and explicit we are, the more we realize that engaging our own learning as professors is also important to engaging students' egos. Noting for students that we are practitioners, too, and letting them comment on our practice opens the conversation fully for unguarded learning.

Conclusion

By intentionally teaching valuable self-evaluation skills and modeling them in a variety of ways, even including aspects of our own performance in the critique, we enfranchise students not only in their own learning processes but in the evolution and improvement of the course itself. We wish to engage students in assessments and evaluations that are meaningful to them in both the present moment and the future. We expect students to move from extrinsic motivation and context (taking a class constructed by someone else) to a position of intrinsic motivation within that context. As professors, we have done that best when we step out of our position of mastery and, instead, model the bumps and spills we incur along the way. The more we trust our students by opening our practice to their input, the less invested we are in having to make the course "work" by ourselves. When we are able to do this, we find that students are more willing to step into their learning with greater commitment and accountability.

References

Boud, D., and N. Falchikov. 2007. "Developing Assessment for Informing Judgment." In *Rethinking Assessment in Higher Education: Learning for the Long Term*, edited by D. Boud and N. Falchikov, 181–197. New York: Routledge.

Clegg, K., and C. Bryan. 2006. "Reflections, Rationales and Realities." In *Innovative Assessment in Higher Education*, edited by C. Bryan and K. Clegg, 216–227. New York: Routledge.

Cox, R. 2009. *The College Fear Factor: How Students and Professors Misunderstand One Another*. Cambridge, MA: Harvard University Press.

Falchikov, N., and D. Boud. 2007. "Assessment and Emotion: The Impact of Being Assessed." In *Rethinking Assessment in Higher Education: Learning for the Long Term*, edited by D. Boud and N. Falchikov, 144–155. New York: Routledge.

Obama, B. 2012. "Remarks by the President in State of Union Address." Washington, DC: The White House, Office of the Press Secretary. http://www.whitehouse.gov/the-press-office/2012/01/24/remarks-president-state-union-address.

Plummer, K. 2003. *Intimate Citizenship: Private Decisions and Public Dialogues*. Seattle: University of Washington Press.

Tan, K. 2007. "Conceptions of Self-Assessment: What Is Needed for Long-Term Learning?" In *Rethinking Assessment in Higher Education: Learning for the Long Term*, edited by D. Boud and N. Falchikov, 114–127. New York: Routledge.

DAVID R. COON *teaches courses in media studies and video production. He researches issues of gender, sexuality, space, and place as they relate to film, television, and advertising.*

INGRID WALKER *researches and teaches courses about contemporary American popular culture. She is writing a book about the cultural impact of U.S. drug prohibition.*

12

Asserting formal authority to address student incivility in the classroom is counterproductive. Rather, professors should employ teaching authority.

The Bruised Ego Syndrome: Its Etiology and Cure

Bruce W. Speck

A theme that emerges from a review of the literature on student incivility in the classroom is the aggrieved faculty response: "What right do students have to question my authority?" In keeping with the thematic intent of this volume, I call this aggrieved response the bruised ego syndrome. I will discuss the etiology of this syndrome, explain why it is an inappropriate response to student incivility, and suggest a cure.

The Source of the Bruised Ego Syndrome

The etiology of this syndrome can be traced to a crucial misunderstanding of types of professorial authority: official authority, subject-matter expertise, and teaching authority (Speck 1998). Official authority refers to the authority vested in professors to preside in the classroom as embodied in a legal contract. Subject-matter expertise is defined as credentialing as certified through degrees and experiences. Teaching authority refers to the ability to help students learn effectively.

The first two types of authority constitute formal authority and appear to be the basis for claims some professors make to explain why students should respect them. For example, Long and Lake (1996) argue that "ethical teaching presumes honesty about the socially structured differences between professors and students. It begins by acknowledging academic inequality, meritocratic elitism, and the possibility for giving pain" (111). In short, according to Long and Lake, professors must assume formal

NEW DIRECTIONS FOR TEACHING AND LEARNING, no. 135, Fall 2013 © Wiley Periodicals, Inc.
Published online in Wiley Online Library (wileyonlinelibrary.com) • DOI: 10.1002/tl.20070

authority to manage the classroom effectively, and the assumption of the mantle of that authority requires role differentiation that stipulates the inequality of students' authority vis-à-vis professors' authority. Unfortunately, Long and Lake assume that professors are up to the task of classroom management because, well, because they are professors and have formal authority. In some mystical way, professorial status confers the type of authority that will ensure that students can learn, if only students will recognize "meritocratic elitism."

Bellah (1999) supports this model of professorial superiority by noting, "It is the teacher, not the student, who knows what the student needs to learn; otherwise, why is the student there at all?" (19). But, of course, to assert that the professor knows what the student needs to learn is not to prove it. What Bellah must be saying, because he would have difficulty defending any notion that professors know the actual state of students' knowledge when they enter the classroom, is that professors have subject-matter expertise and know what is required to be known about their topic if a person is to be considered knowledgeable about that topic. Thus, the bruised ego syndrome focuses on students, not professors, because professors, it is purported, are not the problem. As Benton (2007, C2) laments,

> There are the students who refuse to address us appropriately; who make border-line insulting remarks in class when called upon (enough to irritate but not enough to require immediate action); who arrive late and slam the door behind them; who yawn continually and never cover their mouths; who neglect to bring books, paper, or even something with which to write; who send demanding e-mail messages without a respectful salutation; who make appointments and never show up (after you drove 20 miles and put your kids in daycare to make the meeting).

Hernandez and Fister (2001) proffer a reason that helps explain incivility when they note that college students may see others as peers, not heeding social status in particular contexts. But when they assert, "This is in direct conflict with the drastically different expectations of faculty and staff who assume respect and deference" (Hernandez and Fister, 2001, 56), they assume that faculty and staff expectations are absolutely valid. Are they?

I raise the question because those who argue for deference and respect for teachers appear to base it on title and rank, as though having achieved a certain title or rank entitles one to a certain level of deference, regardless of teaching performance.

Do academic credentials—conferred by institutions of higher education—ensure professional competency in the classroom? Appeals to official authority as supported by subject-matter expertise assume that the credentialing process ensures professional competence in the workplace. However, major flaws in the way professors are vetted for their *teaching*

NEW DIRECTIONS FOR TEACHING AND LEARNING • DOI: 10.1002/tl

responsibilities certainly call into question the validity of the credentialing process. As a system, higher education has not demonstrated its commitment to student learning by the way doctoral candidates are prepared for their pedagogical responsibilities (Bilimoria 1997; Speck 2003; Wilson 1982). Professors are trained as scholars, not as teachers. Somehow (and mystery certainly is at work here) scholars are expected to know how to teach because they are certified as subject-matter experts. The logic of such an assertion is beyond question, evidently, even though the logic is not apparent.

The bruised ego syndrome is exacerbated by failure to accept changes in American culture that have called into question virtually any authority other than personal autonomy. The appeal to personal autonomy is as unfortunate as is the bruised ego syndrome, but a hard, cold look at American culture reveals the crisis of authority. This crisis has multiple sources, and I do not pretend to provide a comprehensive explanation for this crisis. But in fact, people in positions of authority throughout American culture, including professors, violate the stewardship entrusted to them.

A perfectly logical response to transgressions of vested authority is skepticism about the validity of formal authority. In fact, we have long been in the culture of second opinions, as physicians well understand. To bemoan the fact that the leveling of authority has helped create an uncivil society, when academics were on the forefront of protests and attacks in the 1960s regarding the assault on authority, seems a bit disingenuous and too little too late. Academics continue to man the barricades regarding deep distrust of authority, particularly administrative authority, so I find it curious that the very class of people who cry aloud for academic freedom and supposedly promote critical thinking and exploration of ideas on the edge of respectability dis students who question professorial authority. (See Anding 2005, 492, first full paragraph.)

In short, those who espouse the bruised ego syndrome appear to be out of touch with contemporary realities insofar as those realities call for a new paradigm in classroom management. The antagonistic approach advocated by the bruised ego syndrome seeks to superimpose an approach to classroom management that is no longer tenable.

Teaching authority, or a person's ability to teach effectively, is the authority that *should* be at issue in discussing classroom incivility, because how a professor performs as a teacher is critical in addressing incivility in the classroom. To suggest, therefore, that students ought to respect professors based on formal authority alone is to confuse necessary distinctions between credentialing and performance.

In short, the etiology of the bruised ego syndrome can be traced to a long-standing notion of professorial superiority since professors have academic credentials and students ought to respect professors because of the credentials themselves without regard to classroom performance. Professors know what is best for student learning, so the assumption goes, and students ought to assume a position of deference to learned authorities.

Professorial Incivility

The legitimacy of the bruised ego syndrome is further called into question by the fact that professors perpetrate incivility in the classroom. As Boice (1996, 459) notes, "Teachers themselves can be uncivil." Indeed:

> In samplings of core courses at large public universities, as many as a third of faculty treated students with unmistakable rudeness and condescension. In a few cases they physically assaulted students who pressed them for answers or help (Boice, 1986, …), perhaps about as often as students assaulted professors. In many more instances (we do not know the exact figures) professors take advantage of teaching dynamics to sexually and otherwise compromise students. (Boice 1996, 458)

Buttner (2004) agrees, citing research results:

> Numerous students cited instances of instructor rudeness, arrogance, condescension, ridiculing, sarcasm, cutting students off, and putting students down in front of classmates that were embarrassing and humiliating. Citations about these behaviors constituted 107 (53%) of the coded accounts. These behaviors had a chilling effect on some students' motivations. (327)

Others provide evidence of professorial culpability in promoting uncivil behavior (Anthony and Yastik 2011; Benton 2006; Braxton and Bayer 1999; Marchiondo, Marchiondo, and Lasiter 2010). In fact, discussions of academic ethics regarding teaching are meager (Cahn 1986, xi; Rocheleau and Speck 2007, v–ix), presumably because academics have little need to engage in such discussions.

The Need for Reform

It will not do, of course, to lump all professors together. Neither those who claim that reaffirming naked professorial authority is the answer to classroom incivility nor those, like me, who claim that professors do not have clean hands regarding either the historical progress of incivility or the current state of affairs, should act as though the entire professoriate is either innocent or culpable. However, what can be said globally about professorial implication in classroom incivility is that the academy as a whole has fostered a great disservice to students and faculty by failing to adequately address student, professorial, and administrative aspects of incivility on campus. Although this particular chapter can do little more than register a complaint against the academy for a long-standing failure to come to grips with campus incivility, the etiology of campus incivility should be a topic for significant discussion and action, including the legal standing of collegiality (Connell and Savage 2001).

Elsewhere, I have noted the need to prepare graduate students to assume the full-orbed role that professors are expected to fulfill (Speck 2003), but much could be said about the way the academy attracts graduate students with professorial aspirations and the great need to change that selection paradigm so that the match between graduate students' aspirations and market demands for professors is clearly aligned. We continue to overproduce graduate students in the liberal arts for professorial roles, and we continue to focus on scholarship at the expense of pedagogy, as though the reality of academic life for most professors is heavily tilted toward research. We have failed in significant measure to attract and train the types of people who can find adequate satisfaction laboring in the conditions under which most academics work.

One piece of evidence that helps substantiate my claim comes from Boice (1986):

> In my role as traveling consultant on faculty development ... , I estimate that at least 20% to 30% of faculty at many universities and colleges can be described as disillusioned and as unlikely to participate in traditional developmental programs. These individuals are, as a rule, middle-aged, chronically depressed or angry about their jobs, inactive as scholars, isolated and oppositional as colleagues, and unenthusiastic about teaching. (116)

Indeed, Boice's (1991) research regarding the success of new faculty does not promote optimism regarding how we treat fledging members of the profession.

Conclusion

No doubt, students can be uncivil. No doubt, incivility is a cause for great concern regarding student learning. No one really disputes those claims. What I dispute is the professorial attitude that appeals to formal authority as the answer to classroom incivility. Fortunately, a variety of sources provide helpful advice professors can use to establish civility in the classroom (e.g., Baldwin 1997; Braxton and Bayer 2004; Clark 2009; Feldmann 2001; Lippmann, Bulanda, and Wagenaar 2009; Nordstrom, Bartels, and Bucy 2009; Richardson 1999). With the academy's reverence for research, one might hope that those engaged in teaching as a major commitment for their job responsibilities would be engaged in studying such literature for professional growth.

Professors can address incivility appropriately by accepting the reality of student entitlement and seeking to educate students about proper classroom behavior. Students should question authority, and they can do so in ways that will honor civility. The way to heal those with the bruised ego syndrome is to teach them appropriate pedagogical techniques and to assure them that they do have formal authority. What they need to address is teaching authority.

References

Anding, J. M. 2005. "An Interview with Robert E. Quinn, Entering the Fundamental State of Leadership: Reflections on the Path to Transformational Teaching." *Academy of Management Learning & Education* 4 (4): 487–495.

Anthony, M., and J. Yastik. 2011. "Nursing Students' Experiences with Incivility in Clinical Education." *Journal of Nursing Education* 50 (3): 140–144.

Baldwin, R. G. 1997. "Academic Civility Begins in the Classroom." http://www.podnetwork.org/publications/teachingexcellence/97-98/V9,%20N8%20Baldwin.pdf.

Bellah, R. N. 1999. "Freedom, Coercion & Authority." *Academe* 85 (1): 16–21.

Benton, T. H. 2006. "A Tough-Love Manifesto for Professors." *Chronicle of Higher Education* 52 (40): C1–C4.

Benton, T. H. 2007. "Remedial Civility Training." *Chronicle of Higher Education* 53 (36): C2.

Bilimoria, D. 1997. "Management Educators: In Danger of Becoming Pedestrians on the Information Superhighway." *Journal of Management Education* 21 (2): 232–243.

Boice, B. 1996. "Classroom Incivilities." *Research in Higher Education* 37 (4): 453–486.

Boice, R. 1986. "Faculty Development via Field Programs for Middle-Aged, Disillusioned Faculty." *Research in Higher Education* 25 (2): 115–135.

Boice, R. 1991. "New Faculty as Teachers." *Journal of Higher Education* 62 (2): 150–173.

Braxton, J. M., and A. E. Bayer. 1999. *Faculty Misconduct in Collegiate Teaching.* Baltimore: Johns Hopkins University Press.

Braxton, J. M., and A. E. Bayer, eds. 2004. *Addressing Faculty and Student Classroom Improprieties.* New Directions for Teaching and Learning, no. 99. San Francisco: Jossey-Bass.

Buttner, E. H. 2004. "How Do We 'Dis' Students? A Model of (Dis)Respectful Business Instructor Behavior." *Journal of Management Education* 28 (3): 319–334.

Cahn, S. M. 1986. *Saints and Scamps: Ethics in Academia.* Totowa, NJ: Rowman & Littlefield.

Clark, C. M. 2009. "Faculty Field Guide for Promoting Student Civility." *Nurse Educator* 34 (5): 194–197.

Connell, M. A., and F. G. Savage. 2001. "The Role of Collegiality in Higher Education Tenure, Promotion, and Termination Decisions." *Journal of College and University Law* 27 (4): 833–858.

Feldmann, L. J. 2001. "Classroom Civility Is Another of Our Instructor Responsibilities." *College Teaching* 49 (4): 137–140.

Hernandez, T. J., and D. L. Fister. 2001. "Dealing with Disruptive and Emotional College Students: A Systems Model." *Journal of College Counseling* 4: 49–62.

Lippmann, S., R. E. Bulanda, and T. C. Wagenaar. 2009. "Student Entitlement: Issues and Strategies for Confronting Entitlement in the Classroom and Beyond." *College Teaching* 57 (4): 197–204.

Long, G. L., and E. S. Lake. 1996. "A Precondition for Ethical Teaching: Clarity about Role and Inequality." *Teaching Sociology* 24: 111–116.

Marchiondo, K., L. A. Marchiondo, and S. Lasiter. 2010. "Faculty Incivility: Effects on Program Satisfaction of BSN Students." *Journal of Nursing Education* 49 (11): 608–614.

Nordstrom, C. R., L. K. Bartels, and J. Bucy. 2009. "Predicting and Curbing Classroom Incivility in Higher Education." *College Student Journal* 43 (1): 74–85.

Richardson, S. M., ed. 1999. *Promoting Civility: A Teaching Challenge*. New Directions for Teaching and Learning, no. 77. San Francisco: Jossey-Bass.

Rocheleau, J., and B. W. Speck. 2007. *Rights and Wrongs in the College Classroom: Ethical Issues in Postsecondary Teaching*. Bolton, MA: Anker Publishing Company.

Speck, B. W. 1998. "The Teacher's Role in the Pluralistic Classroom." *Perspectives* 28 (1): 19–43.

Speck, B. W. 2003. "The Role of Doctoral Programs in Preparing Faculty for Multiple Roles in the Academy." In *Identifying and Preparing Academic Leaders*, New Directions for Higher Education, no. 124, edited by S. L. Hoppe and B. W. Speck, 41–55. San Francisco: Jossey-Bass.

Wilson, E. K. 1982. "Power, Pretense, and Piggybacking: Some Ethical Issues in Teaching." *Journal of Higher Education* 53 (3): 268–281.

BRUCE W. SPECK is president of Missouri Southern State University in Joplin.

NEW DIRECTIONS FOR TEACHING AND LEARNING • DOI: 10.1002/tl

INDEX

98   FROM ENTITLEMENT TO ENGAGEMENT

Japanese Student Association, 79
Johnson, A. N., 34
Johnson, T. D., 34

Kagan, S. H., 50
Kearney, P. K., 24
Kelly, K., 4, 49
Keniston, K., 9–10
King, M., 15
Knowlton, D. S., 3, 19, 27–28, 39, 63, 64, 72
Knowlton, H. M., 4, 69
Konrath, S., 20, 37
Kopp, T. W., 45
Krueger, J. I., 8

Lake, E. S., 89
Lamott, A., 21
Landreman, L., 77
Language, plain and direct, 38
Lasiter, S., 92
Lavoie, R., 40
Leonard, V., 50
Lessard, J., 37
Lewin, T., 25
Lin, W., 46
Lippmann, S., 3, 41, 43, 93
Long, G. L., 89
Lourey, J., 21, 22

Marchiondo, K., 92
Marchiondo, L. A., 92
Maslow, A. H., 22, 23, 28
Matheson, R., 64
Mayer, J., 75
McConachie, S. M., 14
McDonough, P., 15
McFadden, A., 69, 72
McGlynn, A. P., 55, 56
McKeachie, W. J., 43
McKinney, M., 45
McMorris, R. F., 46
Media-driven lectures, 62–63
Memphis State University, 1
Memphis Tigers, 1
Menand, L., 10, 14
Miley, F., 59
Millennial students: definition of, 1; and engaging in social justice, 75–80; immersive activities and, 50
Miller, K., 31
Miller, M. J., 75, 78
Mills, B. J., 40
Mislan, C., 13, 63

Moffat, M., 8
Moll, L., 55
Morere, L., 75, 78
Morgan, P., 50
Muñiz de la Peña, C., 75, 78
Murphy, C., 27

Narrative pedagogy: across higher education curriculum, 59–60; leveraging self-revelation through, 55–60. *See also* Digital stories
Neff, D., 55
Nelson, C., 15
"New Data on College Students and Overconfidence" (*USA Today*), 31
Newfield, C., 12, 15
Ngai, S., 79
Nilson, L. B., 45
Nordstrom, C. R., 93

Obama, B., 79
O'Brien, E. H., 20
O'Brien, J. G., 40
Out-of-class exchanges: affirming ego through, 69–74

PanHellenic Council, 79
Pardue, K. T., 50
Paul, W., 15
Peterson, D., 44
Petrosky, A. R., 14
Plax, T. G., 24
Plummer, K., 82
Political action: and assignment outcomes, 52; for creating disciplinary thinking and student commitment, 49–53; and implications of immersion assignments, 52–53; and political activities assignment, 50–53; and processed-based planning, 51; written documentation and reflection in, 52
Pollio, H. R., 40
Pope, D. C., 15, 37
PowerPoint, 63
Prentice, M., 75
Prezi, 63
Professor, role of, 34–35

Ramsden, P., 10, 11
Ray, R., 78
Reeves, A. G., 4, 55
Reich, C., 69, 72
Reinhardt, J., 31, 35
Rhee, C., 31

TL134 **Contemplative Studies in Higher Education**
Linda A. Sanders
The complexities of 21st-century life—personal, social, cultural, and environmental—demand thoughtful responses, responses fostered and enhanced through contemplative experience. Contemplative education includes studies of the history, psychology, and social-cultural context of such experience, as well as the development of experiential knowledge through one or more personal practices. The cultivation of a contemplative epistemology, nurtured by attentiveness to and awareness of oneself and one's environment in the present moment, encourages acceptance and awareness of an interdependent, evolving global coexistence between diverse cultures and environments.

Contemplative education has recently emerged in the academy. Although there has been significant published discussion of postsecondary courses and programs that incorporate contemplative views and practices, there have been few studies of relevant curricula and pedagogy. This volume of New Directions for Teaching and Learning integrates research, theory, and practice through a fusion of perspectives and approaches, giving readers the opportunity to review contemplative educational concepts and applications in academic, social, and institutional domains.
ISBN: 978-11187-00983

TL133 **The Breadth of Current Faculty Development: Practitioners' Perspectives**
C. William McKee, Mitzy Johnson, William F. Ritchie, W. Mark Tew
Professional development for faculty has been growing for decades in teaching and learning centers. In the twenty-first century, higher education has entered a startling transformation, and pedagogical philosophy and practice are changing along with the rest of the academy, making faculty development that much more important. Each chapter in this volume of *New Directions for Teaching and Learning* identifies particular areas of opportunity, and although the authors recognize that not every initiative suggested can be implemented by all institutions—circumstances such as institutional mission, available resources, and governance issues will dictate that—it is their hope that every reader will be able to glean details that might provide a spark or fan a flame on campus. As educators themselves, McKee, Johnson, Ritchie, and Tew invite you to consider the challenges, explore the possibilities, and join them on the journey.
ISBN: 978-11186-41545

NEW DIRECTIONS FOR TEACHING AND LEARNING
ORDER FORM SUBSCRIPTION AND SINGLE ISSUES

DISCOUNTED BACK ISSUES:

Use this form to receive 20% off all back issues of *New Directions for Teaching and Learning*.
All single issues priced at **$23.20** (normally $29.00)

TITLE	ISSUE NO.	ISBN
_____	_____	_____
_____	_____	_____
_____	_____	_____

Call 888-378-2537 or see mailing instructions below. When calling, mention the promotional code JBNND
to receive your discount. For a complete list of issues, please visit www.josseybass.com/go/ndtl

SUBSCRIPTIONS: (1 YEAR, 4 ISSUES)

☐ New Order   ☐ Renewal

U.S.	☐ Individual: $89	☐ Institutional: $311
CANADA/MEXICO	☐ Individual: $89	☐ Institutional: $351
ALL OTHERS	☐ Individual: $113	☐ Institutional: $385

Call 888-378-2537 or see mailing and pricing instructions below.
Online subscriptions are available at www.onlinelibrary.wiley.com

ORDER TOTALS:

Issue / Subscription Amount: $ _____

Shipping Amount: $ _____
(for single issues only – subscription prices include shipping)

Total Amount: $ _____

SHIPPING CHARGES:
First Item	$6.00
Each Add'l Item	$2.00

(No sales tax for U.S. subscriptions. Canadian residents, add GST for subscription orders. Individual rate subscriptions must
be paid by personal check or credit card. Individual rate subscriptions may not be resold as library copies.)

BILLING & SHIPPING INFORMATION:

☐ **PAYMENT ENCLOSED:** *(U.S. check or money order only. All payments must be in U.S. dollars.)*

☐ **CREDIT CARD:** ☐VISA ☐MC ☐AMEX

Card number _____Exp. Date_____

Card Holder Name_____Card Issue # _____

Signature _____Day Phone_____

☐ **BILL ME:** *(U.S. institutional orders only. Purchase order required.)*

Purchase order # _____
Federal Tax ID 13559302 • GST 89102-8052

Name_____

Address_____

Phone_____ E-mail_____

Copy or detach page and send to: **John Wiley & Sons, One Montgomery Street, Suite 1200,
San Francisco, CA 94104-4594**

Order Form can also be faxed to: **888-481-2665**

PROMO JBNND